C0-DKN-453

Library of
Davidson College

Coming Out Cold

Coming Out Cold

Community Reentry from a
State Reformatory

A. Verne McArthur
Boston University

Lexington Books
D.C. Heath and Company
Lexington, Massachusetts
Toronto   London

364.3
M116c

Library of Congress Cataloging in Publication Data

McArthur, A. Verne.
  Coming out cold.

  Bibliography: p.
  1. Rehabilitation of juvenile delinquents—United States—Case studies.
2. Reformatories—United States. 3. Corrections—United States. I. Title.
HV9104.M18   364.36'0973   73-15279
ISBN 0-669-91702-8

Copyright © 1974 by D.C. Heath and Company.

All rights reserved. No part of this publication may be reproduced or
transmitted in any form or by any means, electronic or mechanical,
including photocopy, recording, or any information storage or retrieval
system, without permission in writing from the publisher.

Published simultaneously in Canada. 75-4927

Printed in the United States of America.

International Standard Book Number: 0-669-91702-8

Library of Congress Catalog Card Number: 73-15279

To my parents,
Arthur and Thelma McArthur

Contents

Foreword

Unlike the situation with respect to other areas of longstanding social concern, the early 1970s have been a time of "reform" with respect to the workings of our juvenile justice system and its attendant institutions. Exactly why this should be the case—why sudden infusions of money, manpower, and public interest should be focused on the problems of the adjudicated and/or incarcerated "law-breaker" when the unresolved issues of poverty, miseducation, and the unequal application of justice (i.e., the very conditions which spawn and virtually guarantee "criminal behavior") have been placed on the "back burner"—is certainly open to question. Perhaps, as many would like to believe, the resurgence of interest is but another example of the fact that our society, for all its well-documented evils and shortcomings, continues its painful and hesitant evolution toward some higher state of consciousness and collective morality. Or, could it be, perhaps, that this renewed concern has its roots in the Atticas and Soledads that have become endemic in our body politic—in that uncomfortable awareness that the incarcerative experience itself may harbor within it the "dangers" associated with the development of an unanticipated (and unwanted) revolutionary consciousness? In either case, the fact of the matter is that at a time when there is a general pulling-back from "social programs," there is an increasing push being made to significantly alter (and, in some instances, completely do away with) existing correctional facilities for adjudicated youthful offenders.

Dr. McArthur's book might well have been entitled *Catch 22 Revisited*, for a maddening state of affairs surrounds the released offender who seeks to re-enter the community from which he has been separated. Amid the rhetoric of both correctional officials and "helping professionals" concerning the aims and processes of rehabilitation, one clear reality emerges with stark simplicity: the released offender has almost no more of a chance of "making it" (i.e., of becoming a productive, happy and, presumably, nontransgressing human being) than Yossarian had in trying to make sense of the almost pathologically inverted values and behaviors of those who surrounded him and determined his fate. It is, in short, a situation so serious in its implications as to raise some very fundamental questions concerning the part being played by the agencies comprising the "rehabilitative network" in perpetuating—and even exacerbating—the very problems they are rhetorically committed to solving.

This book appears at a time when our nation's highest ranking law enforcement official, Attorney General William Saxbe, has publicly raised the question of the efficacy of rehabilitation for certain incarcerated individuals. Sadly, but perhaps predictably, his concerns with the "myth" of rehabilitation are founded upon an unyielding inclination to view the individuals who "fail to be rehabilitated" as the principal authors of their own continuing outrage. *Coming*

Out Cold is thus a welcome antidote to such simplistic, self-righteous, and "victim-blaming" logic. To be sure, there are a number of myths associated with the process of rehabilitation but, as Dr. McArthur amply and carefully shows us, the greatest myth of all may be the one that presumes a sense of rehabilitative mission, purpose, selflessness and, above all, seriousness, on the part of those entrusted with the life of the offender.

It would be sad indeed if this book were read or interpreted as little more than a passionate personal statement by Dr. McArthur. Quite to the contrary. What Dr. McArthur has done is to systematically isolate, measure, and organize an enormous amount of complex, often perplexing, and elusive data—organize it in such a manner that rhetoric is replaced by reality, argument by fact. As such, he has provided us with a model for what I hope will become a growing, exciting, and accepted field of "advocacy research." But he has also done much more. He has demonstrated that science can be much more than the traditional attempt to study and understand the human condition. It can also seek to change that human condition—and in the process, change itself.

I. Ira Goldenberg

Acknowledgments

I am most in debt to the thirty-four boys and their mothers, the informants of this study, who permitted a glimpse into their lives during a very difficult time. I sincerely hope that their honesty, openness, and trust will be repaid by this book having some small impact on changing those institutional attitudes and practices that in large part shaped their struggles.

My thanks also to the commissioner and the director of programming and planning of the Department of Corrections in the state where the actual research was conducted. They provided the administrative and financial support from the Department of Corrections without which this research could not have been done.

A number of people at Yale University, where this project began as a doctoral thesis, played important roles in making this book possible. Seymour Sarason created the setting, the Yale Psycho-Educational Clinic, which provided me with much of the training, perspective, and support critical to the research and thinking reflected in these pages. I was also very fortunate to have a thesis committee who appreciated and supported what I most wanted to do. My thanks to Ken Keniston, Don Quinlan, Dick Reppucci, Seymour Sarason, and Stan Wheeler. Without the sensitivity, persistence, and commiseration of Neil Watson in sharing the interviewing with me, this research would probably have aborted at several different points. Ira Goldenberg, in his usual humorous and incisive style, provided important guidance and support in my efforts to rewrite this manuscript for publication. More important, he taught me early in my graduate education, through personal example, the meaning of courage and conviction.

Most of all, I wish to express my thanks and personal affection to Dick Reppucci, my thesis advisor, who opened so many doors. My deepest gratitude for your guidance, patience, faith, and willingness to share the risks involved.

A final and special debt is owed to my wife, Leslie, who shared the personal sacrifices of this book for far too long. Without her tolerance—and intolerance—of my trials, tribulations, and not inconsiderable "quirks" as a writer, this book might never have reached completion.

Coming out cold means a lot of searching for what's happening and what's around.

—Bill, a releasee

1 Introduction

This book describes the situation that confronts the released offender as he leaves the restricted world of the prison and seeks to establish a meaningful life for himself in the outside community. Its objective is to understand the problem and issues of community reentry as they are experienced by the offender himself and shaped by the institutional characteristics and procedures surrounding release. It is based on the personal accounts of thirty-four youthful offenders and their mothers, gathered in intensive personal interviews from a week before release to four weeks after release from a state reformatory. It characterizes an experience which, though brief, has considerable personal and social significance, for it will influence whether the offender is able to move from a criminal to a more conventional and productive life.

Let us waste no time in making crystal clear the major finding of this research. The following pages document that the released offender confronts a situation at release that virtually ensures his failure, particularly if failure is measured not simply in terms of recidivism but in terms of the adequacy and meaningfulness of postrelease lives as well. It is a situation that guarantees considerable personal turmoil, limited access to conventional social roles, and little control over personal destiny. It is a situation created in large part by the negligence of the public agencies responsible for managing reentry (the reformatory, the corrections department, probation and parole), and it raises far more serious questions about the behavior of these agencies than it does about the intentions and personal limitations of the individual offender. The negligence of these agencies not only clearly belies their stated commitment to rehabilitation but raises serious questions about the part they themselves play in perpetuating—and even exacerbating—the very problems they are purportedly attempting to solve.

The research reported here not only documents this correctional negligence but also, because of its experiential focus, vividly illustrates the personal costs of this negligence. It constitutes a relatively powerful human statement of the need to change this state of affairs. Yet it must not be allowed to rest at that. Similar criticisms of our correctional system have been raised with increasing frequency from many quarters, inside as well as outside the correctional field. It is no longer possible to raise such criticisms without also asking why this negligence persists in the face of repeated exposure and pleas for reform.

The central question is whether the problems of reform are fundamentally technical or political. That is to say, are the problems ones of ignorance of effective helping strategies, system's problems of communication and definition of responsibility, problems of short-sighted planning, etc.—problems that might be solved by a more effective application of social science technology? Or is the basic problem a more political issue of societal priorities in the distribution of resources and commitment to different classes of people—a problem that demands fundamentally political action? The action implications one draws from data such as that presented in this book will depend considerably on the stance one takes on this issue.

That is where the book is headed. Though it does not purport to resolve the question "Why?", it will suggest different positions that can be, and are, taken on this question, and will formulate its action recommendations in light of the different strategies implied by these alternative stances.

The remainder of this chapter outlines the theoretical and practical context that guided the development of this study and within which its findings have their significance. Chapter 2 presents the particular approach chosen for this research and its rationale, advantages, and limitations. Chapters 3 through 7 provide the core descriptive statement of the problems and processes of reenty as they are experienced by the released offender himself. These chapters describe reentry as it is experienced in process, from facing release from prison, through the transition experience of the first week out, to the issues confronted at the end of the first month of release. Chapter 8 constitutes the major conceptual statement of the meaning of reenty to the offender himself and its potential significance in his life. Chapters 9 and 10 discuss respectively the issues of heroin relapse during reentry and the problems of reentering family relationships. Chapter 11 presents the actual interviews done with one releasee and his mother so the reader can hear in the informants own words the impact reentry has on their lives. The final chapter proposes recommendations for action that follow from different positions on the question of why the criminal justice system persistently neglects the needs of the people it processes.

The Community Corrections Movement

To hear it from the leaders in the correctional field, we are at the beginning, if not in the midst, of a major revolution in correctional practice. This revolution is characterized as leading to the reduction, if not eventual elimination, of the traditional large institutional prison in favor of various smaller community-based treatment centers, halfway houses, and nonresidential programs. It is claimed that this movement represents not simply a programatic change in rehabilitation strategies but a conceptual change as well. The conceptual framework is most clearly stated by the Corrections Task Force of the President's Commission on Law Enforcement and Administration of Justice (Corrections Task Force Report 1967)

The general underlying premise for the new directions in corrections is that crime and delinquency are symptoms of failures and disorganization of the community as well as of individual offenders. In particular, these failures are seen as depriving offenders of contact with the institutions of society that are basically responsible for assuring the development of law-abiding conduct.

The task of corrections therefore includes building or rebuilding solid ties between the offender and the community, integrating or reintegrating the offender into community life. . . . This requires not only efforts toward changing the individual offender, which has been the almost exclusive focus of rehabilitation, but also the mobilization and change of the community and its institutions (p. 7).

In short, the new movement claims to recognize that the central issue of corrections is the impact correctional programs have on the offender's relationship to his community, that this relationship should be the direct focus of correctional work, and that this task is best implemented through correctional programs located in the community of the offender.

"Community corrections" clearly sounds the theme for new directions in corrections. In a 1969 publication entitled "The Future of Corrections" (Conrad 1969), a variety of contributors, including social scientists and prominent correctional administrators, identify and endorse community correctional approaches as the most important new trend in corrections. The overall tone of most contributors is reflected by Schrag (1969): "There can be little doubt that the growing emphasis on community correctional programs is the most distinctive trend in the field today." Indeed, elsewhere Schrag (1971), in a comprehensive assessment of the state of criminal justice in America, asserts that corrections today is entering the "Age of Reintegration." He sees this development as the third major revolution in correctional ideology, following two prior significant shifts in orientation, the first from physical revenge to confinement (with the introduction of the prison in the early nineteenth century), and the second from confinement to rehabilitation after World War II.

Though community corrections remains but an ideal as yet, and though serious questions can and will be raised about the extent to which this rhetoric will translate into reality, it is nevertheless an area of considerable activity and some progress. Currently the most extensive form of community corrections is the use of probation and parole in lieu of imprisonment. About two-thirds of the approximately 1.3 million convicted offenders handled by the correctional system on any given day are being supervised under these conditions (Schrag 1971). Though, in practice, probation and parole provide for more supervision than the supportive services intended in the community corrections model, their use is growing more rapidly than is imprisonment. Thus the large majority of offenders are being maintained in a community status. More significant, a few states have substantially deinstitutionalized their correctional systems, particularly for the juvenile offender. For example, Massachusetts, the first state to introduce training schools for delinquents, has also been the first to virtually eliminate these institutions in favor of a variety of community-based approaches (Bakal 1973). California's Youth Authority handles close to three-fourths of its youthful offenders through various community programs (Warren 1969). At both juvenile and adult levels, community correctional approaches probably represent the most active focus of experimental program development in corrections today (Warren 1972), rivaled only by the increasing application of behavioral principles to correctional rehabilitation.

The purpose here is not to provide a history or comprehensive analysis of the community corrections movement. However, three related but substantially different elements of the community corrections model need to be distinguished. First is the objective of shifting from large, geographically isolated prisons ("total institutions") to smaller, more open programs located in the community. This shift is seen as normalizing the environment of correctional settings, being less disruptive of offenders' community ties, and providing better access to, and articulation with, a variety of community resources. Second is an expansion if not shift in the focus and objectives of the actual correctional work with individual offenders. Reintegration, not rehabilitation, is to be the new focus, meaning that correctional work should not focus exclusively on changing the attitudes and behavior of the offender himself but should help to facilitate more productive social ties between the offender and the community institutions critical to maintaining a law-abiding life (in such areas as employment, education, recreation, housing, and the family). Third, in the model's more ambitious form, correctional work is seen as focusing change efforts directly on community institutions themselves, to make them more responsive to the needs of the offender. Thus, institutional change is to be given equal importance with individual remediation in the focus of correctional work. These distinctions, frequently not clearly made, are critical to assessing the significance of claimed progress toward community corrections. Simple relocation of programs into the community, though important in its own right and probably necessary to the other objectives, by no means ensures the changes in actual correctional work that are the most significant aspect of the community corrections model.

The different types of experimental community correctional programs currently being developed can best be introduced in terms of the particular stage in the correctional process at which they occur. Three basic approaches can be identified. *Diversion* programs seek to avoid incarceration entirely and to intervene either before or immediately after court action. *Institutional community* programs for incarcerated offenders seek to maintain and facilitate community ties despite the isolation of imprisonment. *Community reentry* programs occur at the end of imprisonment and seek to facilitate the transition from prison to effective community lives. Though there are other ways of categorizing community correctional approaches, this schema has the advantage of emphasizing that most do not represent full alternatives to incarceration (avoiding imprisonment entirely), and it acknowledges the reality of the continuing existence of the prison in the foreseeable future.

Diversion programs attempt to circumvent incarceration entirely, with some even directed at circumventing the conviction and labeling process. Pretrial diversion programs intervene between arrest and trial and provide the offender with a variety of manpower and social services to encourage positive community adjustment. Depending on the man's program performance, the court may subsequently decide to drop the charges, thus diverting the man entirely from the criminal justice system. The most frequent post-trial diversion approach is the use of probation. Though in practice probation rarely involves more than supervision, there is experimentation at this stage with increasing the provision of treatment and social services, and with diversion into other community-based programs as a condition of probation, such as halfway houses, group homes, and educational programs.

Institutional community programs occur during imprisonment and represent attempts to build productive community involvement despite the segregation of prison. Release programs involve releasing prisoners during the day, while still technically imprisoned, to attend school, hold jobs, or participate in job-training programs. These programs typically involve only a tiny fraction of a prison's inmates. Furloughs are temporary leaves granted for family visits, job interviews, handling personal affairs, etc. When adopted as a state correctional policy, they can be made available to substantial numbers of inmates, particularly at holiday times. Other institutional programs bring in outside community people for involvement in a variety of educational, recreational, counseling, and advising programs.

Community reentry programs occur at the end of imprisonment and are geared toward facilitating the offender's return to the community. They include institutional prerelease programs, parole, prerelease and postrelease halfway houses, and nonresidential "advocacy" programs. Reentry programs focus both on easing the transition from institution to community and on mobilizing crucial manpower and supportive social services for the offender. Outside of parole, which typically provides little more than supervision, the halfway house is the most common reentry approach and has a substantial history of use with both released offenders and released mental patients. Reentry programs in some ways are the ones most explicitly directed at community reintegration, for they face the task of undoing the effects of institutional isolation as well as facilitating effective community lives.

It is within the context of the community corrections movement that community reentry research has some significance. Community reentry programs will continue to be a major focus for the development of community correctional approaches. Despite the rhetoric of community approaches as the wave of the future, prisons are destined to remain with us for a long time to come. To be responsive to the needs of significant numbers of convicted offenders, community corrections will have to concern itself with their reentry needs. Hence, the development of realistic and effective community correctional approaches will depend considerably on an adequate understanding of the needs and problems offenders confront during reentry.

Community reentry research has a more general significance as well. If community correctional programs are to be directed at more productive impacts on the offender's relationship to the community, as the reintegration ideology implies, it becomes crucial that the development of new approaches be guided by an understanding of the impact *existing* practices have on community relationships in order to ensure that changes are more than superficial. The reentry period is clearly a critical point at which to assess this impact, for the primary task at reentry is reintegration.

Two central issues need much better understanding before we can be confident that any innovations will produce changes beneficial to offenders. First, we need a much more detailed and concrete, as opposed to abstract and theoretical, understanding of the specific ways in which existing correctional structures and procedures contribute to the problems of community reintegration. Change efforts lacking such a detailed understanding of institutional responsibility will most likely generate a proliferation of new programs still directed primarily at *offender* change, while leaving unchanged damaging characteristics of current correctional practice. Second, we need a much better understanding of the *offender's* perspective on both correctional practices and the issues of reintegration. Again, if programs are developed without a real sensitivity to the offender's own point of view, there is little hope that they will really serve his best interests. Hence an understanding of community reentry in terms of the experience of reentry as it is shaped by institutional conditions and procedures should have implications not only for the development of reentry programs but also for other reintegration programs.

Theoretical Context

Historically, most attempts to understand crime and delinquency have sought for causes in the personal and social background of the criminal. Psychological research has generally addressed the question of why some individuals become delinquent and others do not, comparing delinquent and nondelinquent groups on a variety of physical, personality, family, educational, and social dimensions (See Rodman and Grams 1967). Sociologists have generally addressed a somewhat different question: the explanation of differential rates of delinquency in different locations or in different parts of the social structure. They have related the origins of crime and delinquency to such factors as an excess of criminal models in high-crime neighborhoods (Sutherland 1955), status deprivation (Cohen 1966), delinquency subcultures (Miller 1966), and limited access to legitimate opportunity structures (Cloward and Ohlin 1961).

The last several years, however, have witnessed a growing dissatisfaction with this search for general causal explanations of crime and delinquency. Though most researchers maintain that causal theories have some validity when applied to different segments of the criminal population, many have come to believe that the extensive diversity of criminal behavior makes a general application of any common explanation untenable (Warren 1965; Garabedian and Gibbons 1970). Recent thinking and research have further complicated matters by throwing into question some of the critical assumptions underlying much of the previous research. There is, for example, growing evidence of much more middle-class crime and delinquency than was previously believed (Rodman and Grams 1967; Haney and Gold 1973). This finding challenges previous assumptions of the social distribution of criminal behavior, which served as a basis for much research and theory. There is also a growing appreciation that the fact that delinquency and crime are legally defined and identified phenomena creates serious problems for researchers. Variations in law and law enforcement practices introduce arbitrary influences over who gets labeled by the criminal justice system and thus who gets studied as representative of criminal populations.

One result of this dissatisfaction with traditional perspectives has been the emergence of a new approach to understanding crime and delinquency. One element of this new approach is the study of the role played by the criminal justice system itself in the development and perpetuation of crime. Perhaps the most fundamental statement of this position is Becker's: "Social groups create deviance by making the rules whose infractions constitute deviance, and by applying those rules to particular people and labeling them as 'outsiders'" (1963). The implication is that understanding the determinants of this labeling and definition process (the rules, procedures, dynamics, and motives of the labeing system) is as critical to understanding the existence and origins of deviancy as is understanding the individual deviant himself.

This perspective also sees criminal careers as shaped in part by the negative effects of the offender's involvement with the criminal justice system. Offenders are seen as subject to a set of common interactions with the criminal justice system: arrest, court action, institutionalization, release and parole, etc. These are powerful experiences leading to extensive disruption in the offender's life, and it is suggested that it may be fruitful to examine criminal careers in terms of the effects of these common experiences on the offender and his subsequent behavior. The effects of labeling and the public stigma attached to it (Wheeler and Cottrell 1969), the socializing effects on attitudes and behavior, the disruption of community and family ties, are all consequences of involvement with the criminal justice system. This orientation assumes that the criminal justice system, rather than simply being a reactor to "active" deviant behavior, may itself play a substantial role in the shaping of criminal careers, that it may function in ways that produce the deviance it reacts to.

The roots of this orientation can be traced back several years (Tannenbaum

1938; Ohlin 1956). Its major focus has been on understanding the prison culture and organization (Cressey 1961; Cressey 1965; Sykes 1969). It is only within the last few years that the focus has expanded to include other parts of the criminal justice system, such as the courts (Emerson 1969), the police (Wilson 1968), the juvenile justice system (Forer 1970), and parole (Dembo 1971), and has been articulated as an explicit approach to understanding crime and delinquency (Wheeler 1968; Garabedian and Gibbons 1970; Dembo 1971).

A second element of this new approach is a reconceptualization of the nature of criminal careers. Glaser (1964) observes that the careers of criminals move in cycles from criminal to noncriminal involvement and back again. No person is criminal all the time, and even the worst of hardened criminals show periods of months or years of attempts at legitimate activities. Glaser suggests that we should shift from looking for processes that make for persistence in crime to identifying those conditions that promote change from criminal to noncriminal careers and back again.

It is within the context of this new approach that community reentry research assumes its theoretical importance. Release from correctional institutions and reentry into the outside community is a common criminal career experience for large numbers of offenders. It represents an important turning point, for it is a time of choosing between criminal or noncriminal involvement. Hence, it is of some theoretical importance to our understanding of the forces shaping criminal careers. This theoretical orientation underlies the particular focus of the present research on assessing the nature of the release and reentry experience, how this experience is shaped by institutional forces, and its role in determining whether the offender returns to a criminal or noncriminal life style.

Two other more specific theoretical perspectives on crime and delinquency have been important in the development and interpretation of this research. The first can be called "opportunity theory." As articulated most explicitly by Cloward and Ohlin (1961), it combines the notions of differential opportunity and status deprivation. Opportunity theory proposes that under lower-class conditions there is a marked discrepancy between culturally induced aspirations (for social status and material success) and the means available for achieving them. In the absence of legitimate means, crime and delinquency represent attempts to achieve these aspirations through illegitimate means.

Regardless of its validity as a general explanation for the origins of criminal behavior, opportunity theory provides a critical framework for examining the issues of reentry and the direction of postrelease adjustment. The kinds of adjustments made, particularly whether they tend to be conventional or delinquent, will depend considerably on both the aspirations of the offender at release and on the opportunities and resources available for fulfilling them. In order to understand the choices made by releasees, it is critical to assess the relative availability of and support given to opportunities for conventional, law-abiding roles as opposed to nonconventional, delinquent roles. Hence, one focus of this research has been to examine reentry in terms of the aspirations of releasees, the kinds of opportunities available to them at reentry, and the impact of reentry on the utilization of existing opportunities.

The second theoretical perspective, called "self theory" by Erickson et al. (1973), involves a more subjective perspective on the same set of issues. It suggests that an individual's actions are determined not only by the objective availability of alternatives but also by their perceived availability. Self theory postulates that the individual organizes his experiences into a conception of self and of the place of that self in social situations. This conception influences what behaviors and options he considers to be both appropriate and possible for him, and thereby influences his choice of behaviors. During reentry, one of the primary issues is whether the individual will be able to change from a delinquent to a conventional life style. Hence, self theory suggests the importance of examining the reentry experience in terms of its impact on the releasee's own belief in the possibility of change, meaning its impact on his perception of the options available to him and of his own ability to effect changes in those directions.

Glaser's (1964) theory of "differential anticipation" represents an effective integration of these last two perspectives and adds another important dimension. He asserts that most offenders have needs and motivations essentially similar to those of most people: esteem, success, approval, material wealth, security, etc. He argues that whether an individual seeks to meet these needs through legitimate or illegitimate means depends on which means are open to him, psychologically as well as objectively, and from which he anticipates the greatest gratification. Glaser further asserts that the choice of legitimate over illegitimate means depends less on greater immediate rewards than on greater favorable *anticipations* of future rewards. The critical implication is that legitimate opportunities must not only be perceived as available, they also must be perceived as leading to real satisfaction, and to the same kinds of satisfactions that others expect. The theory emphasizes the importance of examining opportunities at reentry in terms of their meaningfulness as well as their availability. If conventional roles are to represent viable choices, they must not only offer the possibility of staying out of prison but a real potential for gratification as well.

The Research Context

No one has defined community reentry beyond the phrase's obvious meaning, so a working definition is offered here. Community reentry most generally refers to a period of transition from being an inmate in prison to the reestablishment of some kind of position in the "free community." Hence, its time span encompasses some period prior to release, the immediate release and transition period, and a postrelease period up to the establishment of some relatively stable community position. The idea of "reentering" or "transition" is basic to the concept and connotes a relatively brief period of time, which should be distinguished from long-term postrelease adjustment. This idea also reflects the general assumption that the movement from prison to the community involves a period of heightened change or flux in several aspects of the individual's life, both psychological and social. What the actual boundaries of this time period are, when it begins before release and ends after release, has not been specifically assessed in any studies. However, prerelease measures have been taken up to three months before release and up to six months after release. The present research indicates a surprisingly well defined reentry period, when measured by the criteria of heightened flux, beginning about three to four weeks prior to release and ending three to five weeks after.

Despite its apparent practical and theoretical importance, there is surprisingly little research on community reentry. There have been numerous attempts to describe and understand prisons and prison culture, and there is extensive research attempting to predict recidivism, or return to prison. Yet few have attempted to understand what happens in between. There are essentially only four major systematic studies in this area: Glaser (1964), Cohen (1972), and Erickson et al. (1973) with adult offenders, and Wheeler (in preparation) with juvenile offenders.

These studies are in substantial agreement as to the major characteristics of the reentry period. The transition from prison to community is difficult to make and is a period of considerable personal turmoil. Most releasees face reentry with little prerelease preparation and seriously lacking in the financial, occupational, social, and emotional resources necessary for a successful postrelease adjustment. The large majority are forced to rely almost exclusively on their own minimal resources, since the responsible public agencies are generally ineffective and insensitive regarding the releasees' needs and problems. Most releasees confront a situation at reentry in which there is little opportunity and even less support for conventional social adjustments. Yet most releasees face reentry with a genuine desire to "make it," to stay out of trouble and certainly to avoid return to prison, and the large majority hold relatively conventional aspirations for their lives: to settle down and become independent and self-supporting. The studies agree that the reentry period has a significant impact on releasees and that even the first few weeks may have an important influence on whether they move in a criminal or noncriminal direction. Unfortunately, it is difficult to avoid concluding from these studies that the choice confronting the released offender at reentry is one between accepting, indeed struggling for, a quite marginal and unsatisfactory "conventional" status in society or a return to a criminal career.

It is impossible to summarize these studies in any more detail than this brief characterization of their major conclusions. What is more important at this point is to indicate the important remaining gaps in research on this problem and the particular contributions made by the present research. First, as indicated previously, there is a real need for an assessment of the ways in which the problems of reentry are shaped by the characteristics and practices of the correctional system itself. The present study looks in particular at the role played by the correctional institution, in this case a state reformatory, both in terms of its more administrative responsibilities of preparation for release and transfer to outside agencies, and also in terms of how the institutional environment influences the inmate's state of mind as he faces release, and how these effects carry over in shaping postrelease experiences and problems.

Second, the present study seeks to characterize the *experience* of reentry from the offender's perspective. Its major addition to the other studies of reentry is its attempt to conceptualize the process of reentry in experiential terms, and more particularly, its attempt to assess the specific ways in which this experience is determined by institutional characteristics and procedures.

Third, within the sparsely studied reentry area, the immediate transition period (the first several days after release), has been even less studied. Yet this period represents the first real contact releasees have with their communities and is likely to have a lasting influence on subsequent events. It is also a critical point at which to examine the influence institutional factors have on reentry experiences, for they may later fade. Most previous studies have examined the immediate transition period in retrospect only, through interviews several weeks later, after memories may have been distorted by intervening events. The present study interviewed the releasees one week after release, in the middle of this period.

Fourth, previous studies all point to age as a critical factor determining the nature of reentry experiences and problems. Though there have been studies of both juvenile and adult offenders, none have focussed specifically on the youthful offender, those between sixteen and twenty-one years old. This is an age of critical transition between youth and adulthood in a variety of respects—educational, occupational, legal, and with respect to personal and community expectations. The present study is directed specifically at this age group and offers an informative comparison with the younger and older groups previously studied.

Fifth, most previous studies have indicated the importance of the family during reentry, particularly for younger offenders, both because it represents the major resource available to releasees and because it is a critical source of either emotional support or emotional stress. In the present study, a family member, the mother, was interviewed directly in order to provide family perspective on the nature and problems of family relationships during reentry.

Finally, the reentry problems of heroin-users have gone almost wholly unexamined, despite the fact that the proportion of heroin-users in institutions for youthful offenders is extremely high. The reentry problems of heroin-users can be expected to be even greater than for others, with reentry stress making abstinence difficult and the drug factor increasing reentry stress. When imprisonment seems to be our society's treatment of choice for addiction, the reentry experiences of heroin addicts demand careful study. Two-thirds of the present sample were heroin-users, most of them having been seriously addicted, and the issues of heroin relapse during reentry are a major focus of this study.

2 Research Methods

Overview

The basic focus of this study was to describe and assess the critical situational and experiential parameters surrounding institutional release and community reentry from a correctional institution for youthful offenders (age sixteen to twenty-one) from the vantage of three points in time and the perspectives of two people. During the first six months of 1970, thirty-four "reentering offenders" and their mothers were intensively interviewed with a semistructured interview form. The boys were interviewed three times: one week prior to release (B1) and one and four weeks after release (B2 and B3). Their mothers were interviewed one week prior to release (M1) and four weeks after release (M2). Hence, for each offender-mother unit, the period of contact represents approximately five weeks and focuses on the short-term aspects of reentry.

Descriptive and Exploratory
Characteristics of the Study

The critical decision was made early that what was needed, given the nature of previous research, was an exploratory, descriptive picture of the reentry situation and the experiences involved in it. Though other studies had been done in this area, none had dealt specifically with this particular age group. Yet age had been found to be a critical determinant of the kinds of reentry situations and experiences encountered upon release. Hence, it was deemed inappropriate to attempt to specify and test hypotheses until more was known in detail and richness about the characteristics of the reentry experiences of the youthful offender.

Furthermore, the decision was made to follow in depth one small set of offenders and their mothers throughout the immediate period of reentry to try to develop a holistic picture of the total process from the perspective of intact units over time. There were no control groups, and no pre- or post release-only groups of subjects for comparison purposes. Though this format raises obvious methodological questions, particularly regarding the impact of the interviews on the reentry process itself (discussed in more detail later), the decision was made on the basis of the need for as personalized and holistic picture as possible, rather than struggling to piece together a complete picture from different people at different points in time. A secondary consideration was the expectation that developing open and trusting relationships would be much more difficult after release than before, making post release-only contacts risky in a small sample study.

Description of the Reformatory

The only reformatory in the state, "R" houses all sentenced offenders from across the state between the ages of sixteen and twenty-one. Its population varies from 300 to 350 and is about 40 percent black. It is located just outside a small town, about an hour's drive from the nearest urban center, making visiting difficult for a large majority of the inmates' families. Though located on a beautifully landscaped sloping hillside, it physically resembles a maximum-security prison, with a huge red brick wall and three guard towers manned round the clock. Inside, the major living quarters consist of a huge, vintage, seven-tier, steel-barred cell block located in a gray, drafty, cavernous hall about the size of a football field. There is also a new three-floor wing with more individualized rooms (though centrally locked) where inmates nearing release are housed if on good behavior. Toilet facilities are relatively adequate, and the whole institution is clean to the point of seeming antiseptic. There are twenty solitary confinement cells for disciplinary purposes, some with mattress and toilet and some without, and both types are typically half filled. Within the walls are also located three multifloor shop buildings, the administration unit, auditorium, dining hall, and a large grassy outdoor recreation area. There were three counselors, mostly inaccessible to inmates,[1] a small but accessible vocational rehabilitation unit, and the part-time services of a doctor, dentist, and psychiatrist.

Length of sentences ranged from a couple of months up to five years, although few were kept that long. At the time of the study, the majority of inmates never set foot outside the institution walls during their period of incarceration. Inmates spent half the day working in some capacity at 25 cents a day (laundry, maintenance, making license plates, repairing furniture, etc.) and half the day in the educational program. In addition, there were two hours of daily recreation. The over-all tension level was generally low, though there were occasional serious fights and occasional suicide attempts.

During the period of the study, some changes were occurring in the institution. A somewhat promising educational program was being developed, lending some excitement and individualized attention to the largely anonymous environment. Visiting hours were extended to evening hours (still limited to four hours a month with weekends and holidays excluded), mail censorship was

---

[1] Shortly after the study began, the counselors' offices were moved from the main hall connecting the cellblock with the dining and work areas, where inmates had been able to drop in to see their counselors, to the basement. The stated purpose of the move was to allow the counselors to do their "paperwork" without interruption from the inmates.

dropped, and in a number of ways some of the rigidity of the institution was being modified. A limited vocational training program was being run with a nearby technical training school.

Sample Characteristics

Boys[2]

Every offender due to be released directly from the state reformatory between January 1 and May 15 of 1970 was considered a potential subject providing he:

1. Had a minimum length of stay (LOS) at the reformatory of at least three months.
2. Was returning to a town with a population of at least 25,000. Pilot interviews indicated important differences in reentry experiences between urban and rural communities. The smaller cities represented in this study were closely associated with large urban areas. Hence the study represents exclusively an urban population.
3. Was returning to some kind of family residential situation. (Family situations could, in addition to parental families, include foster families and residence with relatives or siblings. The condition was only that they be seriously planning to live in one of these situations immediately after release.)
4. Was English-speaking. After one pilot attempt, Spanish-speaking boys were excluded due to the language barrier with their parents.
5. Was being released in standard fashion. A handful of offenders being released through the one small prerelease program associated with a city jail were excluded on the basis that their situation and experiences would be different and cloud the typical reentry picture.

It was judged that 75 percent of the boys in the reformatory met these conditions, and thus should provide meaningful generalizations for significant numbers of boys.

The major demographic characteristics of the research sample of thirty-four were:

1. *Condition of postrelease supervision:*

Condition	No. of Ss
Parole	14
Probation	11
Discharge (no postrelease supervision)	9

[2] "Boys" is obviously a misleading term with which to refer to males between the ages of sixteen and twenty-one, especially those who have been in prison. Yet there is no satisfactory term. "Men" isn't right either, "youths" sounds like summer camp, "young men" like Sunday school, and "guys" doesn't do for a scientific paper.

2. *Race*   No. of Ss

    White   18

    Black   16

3. *Drugs:*   No. of Ss

    Former addicts   21

    Nonaddicts   13

4. *Mean age:* 19.72 years.

5. *Mean educational level:* 9.79 years.

6. *Mean LOS:* 7.74 months.

7. *Mean number of previous incarcerations:* .88

The only dimension on which there were significant differences in the other variables was release status, where there were differences in:

Release Status	No. of Ss	Average LOS	Previous Incarcerations	
			One or More	None
Parole	14	10.57 Mo.	6	8
Probation	11	4.45 Mo.	3	8
Discharge	9	7.33 Mo.	8	1

There were no significant differences between blacks and whites nor between addicts and nonaddicts on any of the above variables.

Postrelease Supervision Conditions

Parole These boys have been released to the authority and supervision of the state parole system. They must report periodically to their parole officer and are subject to all the regulations of the parole system. They have not been discharged from the reformatory, as they are legally serving the final portion of their sentence on the outside.

Probation These boys have been officially discharged from the reformatory as having completed their sentences but are released to the authority and supervision of the state probation system in lieu of incarceration for some offense other than the one for which they served time at the reformatory. Regulations and supervision tend to be less strict than parole, but it does involve reporting periodically to a probation officer and being subject to probation regulations.

Discharge These boys have served their full sentence and have no other remaining obligations to the criminal justice system. They are officially discharged from the reformatory and are subject to no postrelease supervision.

Families

For a number of reasons, the mother was chosen as the representative of the family to be interviewed. First was the expectation that in many cases there would be no father present in the home. This turned out to be true in 50 percent of the cases. Second, it was felt that the family interview should be with the same parent for all subjects if at all possible. Third, it was expected that in most cases the mother would be the easiest to contact and probably the most open to being interviewed. In only two cases was it necessary to interview the father, one because the stepmother spoke only Polish and the other because the mother was very sick. If the boy was not living with his parents (e.g., with relatives instead), the predominant woman in the residence was interviewed. In only five cases were the interviews done with someone other than one of the natural parents. As 80 percent of the family contacts were the natural mother, the word *mother* will be used in the text in referring to all such contacts. Occasionally, *parents* or *family* might be used in some discussion if the mother's data is being taken as representative of the larger family.

Subject Cooperation

Cooperation exceeded all expectations. Each boy-mother unit involved a total of five interviews, three with the boy and two with the mother. Any unit was retained in the analysis if three of the five interviews were completed. It was necessary to drop only two cases for failure to meet this criterion, and only five of the thirty-four retained units have missing interviews. One hundred of the 102 possible interviews with the boys were completed, and 64 of the 68 possible interviews with the mothers were completed. In no cases did both boy and mother refuse the same interview, and in all cases there is an interview from each of the three contact times. Credit this impressive cooperation mostly to the willingness of the subjects and partly to the skill and persistence of the interviewers.

Description of the Interview

Interviewers

There were two interviewers, the author and an assistant. Each interviewer interviewed half of the boys and the mothers of the other half of the boys. This split was to assure all involved of the confidentiality of what they said and without exception was successful. Both interviewers were white, male college graduates in their twenties.

Interviews

The interviews themselves were semistructured, containing a mixture of open-ended questions, specific short-response questions, and three-point scales and ranking questions. They took between 1½ and 2 hours to administer, with the interviewer writing the responses himself on the mimeographed interview form. All of the interviews were conducted in the subjects' own homes with the exception of the boys' prerelease interview, which was done in the reformatory library. In all but a handful of cases conditions of privacy were acceptable.

Instructions to the Boys

The presentation of the study to the subjects was critical in achieving cooperation and honesty and warrants some discussion. The interviewers presented themselves as university psychologists doing research for the Department of Corrections. This gave us legitimate but independent status; we weren't immediately categorized as bad. We indicated that we, and the Department of Corrections, were concerned about the problems of leaving a reformatory and trying to make it on the outside, and wanted to figure out how to do something about it. We said that most people never talked about the problems with the actual people going through them. In this sense, they were the "experts," and we wanted them to tell us what it was like so things might improve for other guys getting out later. We told them we would pay them for talking with us: a total of $5 for the first two interviews and $7 for the final interview. We made explicit our two actual reasons. First, what they had to say was critical to understanding and dealing with these problems, so they should be paid for it. Second, we wanted to insure that they came for all three interviews. The payment went up for the last interview because we felt that for a number of reasons they might be reluctant to talk to us, and we wanted to make it worth their while to do so. We tried to convince them of confidentiality by indicating that we would report only group data, that we had no interest in reporting individual data, and that we knew if we ever did, the word would get around and we'd be finished—no one would be honest with us.

We explained the interview arrangements with their mothers and showed that neither would hear what the other said. We also said that the main goal was to understand what getting out was like, but that sometimes guys found it helpful to talk with someone. We let them ask questions and then proceeded with the interview.

These instructions seemed to give us a legitimate but trusted status within the institution, to convince the boys that we really did care about what they had to say and would not abuse the data, and were basically "all right" guys to talk to. They seemed to respond positively to the idea that they had something to contribute to a relatively important enterprise.

Instructions to the Mother

The mother received essentially the same instructions, except that they were never offered payment; the payment to their sons was explained to them. Though the same indications concerning help were given, more mothers than boys probably had initial fantasies of receiving some kind of help.

Honesty

The interviews, particularly the first two, seemed to be eagerly welcomed by all but one or two boys as a chance to talk with a sympathetic listener who had virtually no influence over what happened. The extent to which the boys revealed their postrelease drug use and delinquent activities was impressive, indicating high levels of trust and little attempt to conceal dangerous information. When concealment did seem to be a problem, it was in areas where it seemed that the boys were being dishonest with themselves, mostly regarding family concerns. Having the mother's interview data usually allowed some basis for a more accurate assessment in these cases. On the whole, however, most boys seemed quite open in all areas covered.

Honesty and openness on the part of the mothers was not quite as high as with the boys. For very real and understandable reasons, they tended not to buy into the "importance" of the research as much as the boys did, and were occasionally somewhat resistant as it became clear that the interviews really weren't going to be of direct benefit to them. However, most of them seemed to respond positively, often eagerly, to the chance to talk with *anyone* about issues often very troubling to them. A few cried during the interviews, and there was little difficulty with most in arranging a second interview. For the most part, the level of openness and honesty in these interviews seemed acceptable.

Issues of Data Analysis

A number of quantified and quantifiable variables were included in the interviews which provide numerical data for standard statistical analyses. When appropriate and meaningful, analyses including correlations, t tests, analyses of variance, and chi squares, are presented and provide at times a solid and important basis for conclusions.

A major portion of the statistical analysis will be referred to as the intercorrelation analysis. All of the quantifiable variables from each interview (B1, M1, B3, etc.) were intercorrelated. In many instances, redundant and highly correlated variables were collapsed and the intercorrelations were redone using the new variables. Various relevant cross correlations were run between different sets of interviews (B1 vs. B2, M1 vs. M2, etc.). For the most part, the extensive effort required in this analysis far exceeded the value of the results. Yet it was used as a check on other more descriptive conclusions, and occasionally findings from the intercorrelation analysis proved quite provocative and helpful. The findings from this analysis will be reported on a very selective basis when they seem to make sense and have importance in the general interview context.

By far the richest and most fruitful basis for understanding the reentry experience was the answers and comments to the open-ended questions. A variety of more common-sense descriptive approaches were devised in attempts to capture and assess what the subjects seemed to be saying. These approaches will be described as they arise in the text.

One issue, however, warrants more consideration at this point. Subjects, as expected, varied widely in their insightfulness and articulateness, and somewhat in their openness. With respect to open-ended questions, this raised real problems in using frequencies or other "head counts" as bases for conclusions. Generally, if the comments of a handful of subjects seemed to make a great deal of sense in understanding a particular issue, the attempt was made to go back to the data of other subjects and devise some way of looking at it to see if the basic notion could be supported or disconfirmed, particularly considering the context of the question and the expected likelihood of others making similar responses. In some cases where this proved fruitless, the insight is simply offered as one that makes a great deal of sense to the author but can be neither confirmed nor disconfirmed directly in the data.

Advantages and Limitations
of the Study

The main advantage of the study relative to other possible approaches is in the detail and complexity with which the release and reentry phenomena have been viewed. Contacts at three points in time and with both mother and son have provided a rich and personalized source of data from which to attempt to understand the experiences and processes involved. The author has been in every subject's home, searched diligently through each neighborhood attempting to find it, and from one perspective or the other has followed the changes of each subject from institution to street. The attempt was made to follow people in their wholeness and complexity and hopefully has succeeded more than failed.

There are limitations that should be explicitly recognized. The study concerns one institution at one point in its history. There is little, however, that suggests that it is atypical. A relatively thorough search of the literature failed to turn up anything that indicated that either the state correctional system or the reformatory itself were much different from other state systems and reformatories. Discussions with several researchers and correctional personnel with wide exposure to corrections in this country supported this conclusion. In addition, several knowledgeable people have read the manuscript and indicate that the state of affairs it describes is quite typical of correctional practice.

The sample chosen for the study does not represent boys or families from small towns, nor does it represent boys who are going to be living in nonfamily situations. Preliminary indications are that release experiences of these boys may be somewhat different.

A major issue is whether the study itself had some impact on the phenomena being studied. Since there are no pre- or postrelease-only groups of subjects, such an impact is difficult to assess directly. On the one hand, one's strong sense is that the social, institutional, and individual factors involved are quite powerful, and that three to five interviews will have little impact on what happens. (As a practitioner, I could only wish they would.) On the other hand, much of the phenomena of interest are the relatively transient experiences of the immediate reentry period, and it is much more possible that a study format that provides the only individual present during this whole period could have some effect on both boy and family. In some final questions directed at this issue, both boy and mother indicated that while they found the interviews both interesting and enjoyable, they didn't think they changed a thing that happened. Such information is limited but at least is consistent with the impression of minimal impact. It also seems true that for the most part interviews that provide a supportive relationship and stimulate reflection would tend to minimize the shock and/or difficulties of reentry. If true, the impact may be in a conservative, rather than liberal direction.

A study such as this, which seeks to embed itself meaningfully in the on-going lives of people and institutions, requires substantial trust, cooperation, and support from many people. A brief discussion of the conditions critical to realizing this support is an essential part of the methodology. Most important, it grew out of a substantial history of experience and work in the area on the part of a number of people critical to whatever success was achieved. It would never have been possible had it sprung newborn only from the mind of the author.

In the first place, the study was embedded in an on-going service project[3] to the state department of corrections. The relationships developed around services provided to the department in the preceding year were fundamental to the trust, cooperation, and financial support from the department that made a study of this type at all feasible.

---

[3] A faculty-student team (directed by Dr. N. Dickon Reppucci) from the Yale Psycho-Educational Clinic had been working in the Department for a year before the initiation of this study.

In the second place, the nature of the current investigation and the issues examined grew out of the author's three years of prior training experiences in some way related to issues of juvenile delinquency and corrections, including one year in the Department of Corrections itself. These experiences contributed to the development of a study whose issues seemed to make sense to most people involved and also provided the groundwork of initial relationships with a variety of people needed for effective implementation of this study.

And finally, both the author and the assistant interviewer had had substantial experience in human service programs. These experiences had taught them a great deal of respect for, and at least some sensitivity to, the needs of people struggling with difficult problems and had taught them as well the kind of patience and persistence needed to gain the effective cooperation of people in real community contexts.

3   Facing Release From Prison

If there's anything these guys know, it's their release date.
Sgt. Brockton, guard

You wonder if they are really going to let you out.
Jim Duncan, inmate

The first questions that consistently seem to intrigue most people, particularly psychologists, about issues of release from correctional institutions are those that have to do with prerelease anxiety, institutional dependency, and the question of whether there is a tendency for inmates to foul up their release so that they don't have to face the uncertainties of life on the "outside." It is an interest buttressed by at least occasional observations of such apparently "self-defeating" behavior and is an issue that has been recognized in mental hospitals for some time.

The assumption guiding this research, however, has been that these and other feelings and behaviors associated with release are not "innate inmate" tendencies nor simply fears of an uncertain future but are responses and reactions to the situational characteristics of the prerelease situation itself. If one takes this assumption seriously, the *first* task is to assess what these situational characteristics are. That is, the assumption is made that one cannot understand the psychological reactions associated with release without first understanding the characteristics of the institutional context and practices in which they occur. Hence, the major task of this chapter will be to characterize the prerelease institutional context and to assess its impact on the prerelease experience.

The discussion in this chapter is based on three sources of data. The primary information comes from the first interview with the boys, which was done in the reformatory institution itself a week before release. At this interview, details of events during the final week of incarceration could not be covered. A number of questions were included in the B2 interview, a week after release, asking the boys to discuss the final events of their stay. Finally, interviews and discussions were held with a variety of the institutional staff as well—correctional officers, counselors, administration officials—in an attempt to understand from the institutional side the release procedures involved.

Institutional Characteristics of
the Prerelease Situation

Four institutional characteristics play a major role in shaping the prerelease experience.

1. Many institutional conditions create serious uncertainty about the actual release date itself.
2. Institutional supports are seriously inadequate for effective release planning and preparation.
3. Nonoverlapping spheres of responsibility at release hinder both prerelease preparation and transfer from institution to outside agencies.
4. Transition from the institution to the community is very abrupt.

1. *Many institutional conditions create serious uncertainty about the actual release date itself.*

There is a major contradiction between staff and inmate feelings about the certainty of release dates. A number of staff stated unequivocally that if there is anything an inmate knows for sure, it is his release date. Yet 50 percent of the boys report that the first thing they did on the morning of release was to ask a guard to verify that they were supposed to get out that day.

Two major institutional sources of uncertainty about release can be identified: "planned uncertainty" and "systems' confusion." "Planned uncertainty" refers to those flexibilities deliberately built into procedures for determining and modifying release dates. Indefinite sentences give great latitude to parole boards as to date of release and raise the spectre of repeated negative decisions. Parole dates already granted by the board may be delayed because parole officers fail to approve postrelease plans (job, residence, etc.). Time-off for good behavior can be lost at any time for disciplinary infractions. These deliberate uncertainties can lead to change in the release date right up to the day of release itself and mean that no release is really certain until it actually happens.

"Systems' confusion" refers to some error or confusion about the release date on the part of the institution, a confusion that can take several days or weeks to get ironed out. At some point the boy either discovers that the staff is unable to tell him exactly what his release date is or he is told that a mistake has been made and his date had been changed. Actual changes range from a few days to several weeks, but the crucial point is the confusion. These problems represent inept operations of the system, something the inmate has even less control over than disciplinary infractions or parole plan approval. Such problems communicate not only the possibility of change, but the possibility of error.

More than half of the sample were affected by either or both of these sources of uncertainty. Disciplinary actions delayed release dates in six cases, three within the last week. Eleven boys were victims of system's confusion, which often remained unresolved for a number of weeks. No parole plans failed to gain approval, but of the fourteen boys (40 percent) being paroled, in *no* cases were the plans (and hence the release date) officially approved before the morning of release itself. In fact, the possibility of problems persists right up until the moment of walking out the door itself. Seven boys discovered on the day of release that their names had been left off the day's list of releases. Though this was shortly rectified, these boys suffered several moments of no small panic.

More important than objective measures regarding the percent of cases affected is the level of subjective uncertainty. Many of the difficulties do not inspire confidence that the system will work properly in one's own case. In a system not known for the depth of its concern with the individuals living in it, it takes very few examples of the following kind to convince an inmate that things can go badly wrong.

Example 1. Some three months prior to our interview, Carl had spent a week in solitary confinement for stealing doughnuts from the kitchen where he worked, to give friends at Christmas. He thought that that had been the end of it. What he had not been told was that he had also lost a week of "good time" for his offense, which meant that he was to be released a week later than he thought. He discovered this during the interview from the discrepancy in our information. He thought he was to be released *the next day* and, were it not for the interview, would not have discovered the mistake until the following morning, when he expected to be leaving. His mother, who was coming to pick him up, had not been notified either. Needless to say, he was extremely upset, and it is to his considerable credit that he didn't earn himself another week or more in the "hole."

Other data indicates that this situation does indeed generate considerable subjective uncertainty. To open questions concerning reactions to nearing release, more than a third of the boys said something like, "You wonder if they are really going to let you out" or "You're really afraid that something is going to happen to screw up your release." Again, the most dramatic evidence of the subjective uncertainty is that on the morning of release, fully half of the boys asked a guard to verify that they were due for release that day. They did not seem convinced that the system would actually make it happen.

Yet throughout all of this, the institution acted as if there were no uncertainty in the release process. There were no systematic procedures to verify the release date with inmates after it had been determined. It was entirely possible for parolees to serve out their final six weeks with no official verification and for those on definite sentences to *never* have their release date verified by the staff. When asked to indicate the last time their release date had been verified by any institutional staff member, only eleven (a third) reported verification within the last month of release, and none within the last week.

There seemed to be two ways of dealing with this situation of uncertainty. Some boys responded by energetically checking and rechecking their release dates. The majority, however, seemed to follow the maxim of remaining as invisible as possible and waiting it out. In all probability, most boys did some of both—checking out dates until they thought they were set and then waiting out the end as unobtrusively as possible.

2. *Institutional supports are seriously inadequate for effective release planning and preparation.*

Not one boy received what could be at all considered adequate release-focused counseling, directed either at anticipating adjustment difficulties or at forming concrete postrelease plans. About a third received job-related counseling from the vocational rehabilitation staff, and a handful of others spent perhaps up to an hour in informal discussions with a teacher, counselor, or volunteer from outside. Yet none of this resembled serious planning or preparation, and close to a half did not speak with anyone prior to release. The three counselors were themselves quite open in admitting that they felt little responsibility for helping inmates with release issues and did so only when approached with a specific problem.

The effect of this lack of help is evident in other areas:

Family contact. As late as a week before release, a third of the boys were not sure that their families knew they were coming home soon. Staff indicated they felt no responsibility to notify families of release and had done so in only two cases when specifically requested by the inmate. Eleven boys still had no definite arrangements for transportation home.

Employment. Only five boys had jobs definitely lined up before release, and only eleven others had even tentative arrangements made. Eighteen boys had nothing in mind in the way of employment. This situation existed despite the fact that thirty of the thirty-four indicated they wanted to work upon release, despite the fact that working is a regulation of both parole and probation to which twenty-five boys were being released, and despite the fact that gainful employment is clearly considered a cornerstone of successful adjustment by the outside society.

Preparation for parole or probation. Over 70 percent of the boys were being released to probation or parole. Of fourteen boys released to parole, only three knew their parole officer's names before the morning of release, and none had had any contact with him. Only five received any instruction or explanation about parole regulations prior to release. All did sign a written statement of parole regulations on the morning of release. Of the eleven to be released on probation, eight assumed they would have the same officer as they had before incarceration, but had not been told. Only three had had any contact (all through letters) with him. None had had any instruction or explanation of probation regulations prior to release. As part of release they are supposed to sign a form notifying them of their probation status, but six of the eleven said they signed no such form. *Two boys were released without even knowing that they were still supposed to be on probation.*

What should be abundantly clear by now is that the institution did very little to pave the boy's return to the community. Very little groundwork was laid to facilitate a successful readjustment after release, whether one looks to personal preparation, family relationships, employment arrangements, or parole and probation preparation. Indeed, one can view the prerelease institutional situation as one that seriously *interfered* with adaptive preparation. Boys were typically forced to rely on their own resources to make their own arrangements. Yet contact with the outside world is seriously restricted—geographically, procedurally, and psychologically—making this an almost impossible task.

3. *Nonoverlapping spheres of responsibility at release hinder both prerelease preparation and transfer from institution to outside agencies.*

There is little overlap in the spheres of responsibility for the offender as he moves between two different parts of the system during release. The institution is concerned with managing the inmate during imprisonment, and parole and probation are concerned with managing what happens after he leaves. Neither side deals with the transfer period. The institution does little beyond the required mechanics of paperwork of releasing the inmate. Though parole is responsible for helping make postrelease arrangements, they rarely do so before release and only minimally afterwards. The reformatory staff openly admitted that frequently they and the parole officers each insist that the other has responsibility, with the result that nothing gets done. Even the simple administrative transfer got mishandled.

Example 2. Transfer to parole supervision was managed more effectively than transfer to probation because greater overlap in responsibility insured better administrative coordination. Parole and the reformatory have responsibility for the boy around the same offense and sentence. Probation's responsibility, however, derives from an offense and sentence prior to, and different from, that for which the boy is at the reformatory. Hence, whereas the parole board decides the actual release dates of parolees, probation resumes interrupted responsibility only *after* the boy has been officially discharged from the reformatory.

Very different levels of coordination result. In the case of parole, local offices are notified of the release date, parole officers are assigned to each individual, and every boy knows he will be on parole and that he must report immediately upon release. All fourteen parolees had reported to their officers within a week after release. The case of probation is entirely different. At no point is probation ever notified of the boy's actual release date—not at admission, not when changes occur, not even at release. Notification to inmates of their probation status breaks down. Less than half signed the required notification form, and two boys were released without knowing they were on probation. Four of the eleven on probation had not yet contacted their officers as of a month after release, and neither had their officers contacted them. It is likely that the officers did not know the boys were out of jail.

Example 3. The vocational rehabilitation service at the institution faced a similar problem created by nonoverlapping spheres of responsibility. Of all the reformatory's staff, these counselors were the most concerned with helping inmates make and implement plans, though their mandate was restricted to those being released to parole. They made serious efforts to assess job skills, provide job information, and help inmates make concrete plans. But they were administratively and geographically restricted to forwarding inmates' files to regional offices for implementation. Establishing a relationship with the regional office rested on either the boys own initiative or depended on a regional officer who had never met the boy. Issues of communication, coordination, and trust all arose and vocational rehabilitation counselors at the reformatory estimated that plans were effectively implemented in no more than 30 percent of their cases, a frustrating situation to them.

Less official helping resources—families, community agencies, friends—who might potentially be of help in facilitating transfer from the institution, confront similar problems. Administrative policies (e.g., who may visit inmates and how often) typically interfere with any such group establishing effective prerelease contact with the inmate and laying any groundwork prior to release.

4. *Transition from the institution to the outside community is very abrupt.*

This is so obvious that it can all too easily be taken for granted. Except for five boys who had been home for one weekend on a newly begun furlough program, these inmates had not set foot outside the institution prior to walking out the front gate on the morning of release. They were completely inside one day and completely out the next. This abrupt transition from one environment to another creates difficult postrelease adjustment problems. It also affects the prerelease period. Because of its all-or-nothing nature, the anticipated event of release itself becomes a focus of heightened anxiety and excitement and assumes a dominating influence over prerelease feelings in ways that interfere with effective release preparation.

The Psychology of Getting Short

Inmates have their own term, "getting short," to refer to the time of nearing release, approximately the last month before release. The predominant characteristic of this period is that "doing your time" becomes significantly harder than before (as reported by about 75 percent of the sample). Thoughts of getting out dominate the inmate's thinking, and time drags by in what sounds like an interminable and excruciating limbo:

It's all you can think about—you just count the days."

"It seems like the day will never come. You know that it is just a week more, but you feel that it's so close anyway, why can't they just let me out now?"

Tension increases considerably. More than half reported increased tension around guards and other inmates and were afraid of being provoked (either deliberately or unintentionally) into misbehavior that would delay release. Many reported wondering whether the reformatory was really going to let them out or not.

The over-all prerelease situation can best be characterized .in terms of two parameters that integrate both the institutional characteristics and psychological reactions.

"Getting out" becomes a major task in its own right, a task that absorbs most of the energy and interest of the inmates during this time. This is true whether the task involves actively riding herd on one's release date and the changes it can undergo, whether it means remaining as inconspicuous as possible and simply living out the uncertainty, or whether it means enduring the tensions preceding release. The management of these tasks simply dominates the whole prerelease picture and seems to make it almost impossible to engage in other thinking and planning that would prepare one for release.

In the absence of institutional supports, making plans and anticipating the future are not adaptive responses. This is best put by one of the inmates: "Why should I plan? I can't do anything about it while I'm here anyway. It just gets frustrating and depressing." The institution does not facilitate acting on plans or laying groundwork for the future; indeed, it significantly interferes with these activities. Really trying to make and implement plans typically becomes a frustrating exercise in futility. Furthermore, in the absence of counseling relationships, a realistic assessment of future problems with family, friends, drugs, or personal adjustment is most likely to generate serious feelings of depression and fatalism. Given these constraints, the most adaptive response is to avoid to the best of one's ability a realistic assessment of the future. The inmate's major resource in this situation is best stated by one of them: "What you have to do is *think positive.* You can't dwell on your problems or you lose the only thing going for you."

In addition to insuring the absence of concrete plans and arrangements as ground work for successful postrelease adjustment, this prerelease situation has a definite impact on the psychological frame of mind with which inmates approach reentry. First, in the absence of supports for concrete planning, plans tend to be restricted to "good intentions." Many boys said that their plans were to "go straight this time" or "stay out of trouble" or "keep a job." Since such global good intentions are frequently heard by others with an all-too-familiar hollow ring, it is very important to be aware that the constraints of the prerelease situation itself frequently restrict plans to this form.

Second, a situation that restricts plans to good intentions exacerbates feelings of uncertainty about the future. Inmates frequently share others' skepticism about their ability to follow through on their intentions. They often know how differently they may feel about things as soon as they get out. This sets up a vicious circle of self-doubt: "I think I know that I really want to try this time, but then I begin to wonder if I will still feel the same when I get out there—and my mind just starts going in circles."

What becomes very clear is what should be obvious: prison is not a place where one can test out good intentions. There simply are no opportunities to succeed or fail in the kinds of behaviors needed for successful adjustment on the outside, and this leaves the inmate very uncertain about his ability to succeed.

Third, the major concerns in inmate's minds are somewhat distorted. In response to questions concerning their worries about life on the outside, two-thirds reported one of three kinds of major concerns: Will I be coming back here? Will I slip back into old habits? Will I use drugs again? All three translate "Will I make it or not?" The point is not that this is an unrealistic concern but that it is in such an all-or-nothing form and has not been made more specific, concrete, and manageable. It creates a reentry period in which the stakes are very high, since any short-term difficulties or failures will be interpreted as significant signs of one's inability to "make it." It contributes to a relatively low tolerance for the inevitable difficulties and setbacks of postrelease adjustment.

Fourth, the primary tasks of adjustment anticipated by inmates (as reported in response to the question of what they had to do in order to "make it") are formulated in terms of *avoiding* trouble. More than two-thirds of the responses referred to *avoiding* former friends, staying *off* drugs, keeping jobs in order to stay *off* the streets and *out of* trouble. The basic perceived task for most was the essentially negative one of protecting themselves from circumstances that might get them back into trouble. This turned out to be one of the major unrealities of prerelease expectations.

Fifth, at some level, most seem to feel that their only resource during reentry will be their own will power. They feel that unless they are able to "control their minds," "think positive," or keep a "strong mind," they will have lost the only real thing they have going for them.

Finally, the prison environment and the prerelease situation distort positive anticipations about release and the future. The data show that these anticipations were overwhelmingly dominated by pleasures reflecting freedoms they had been deprived of in prison. Being free from guards telling them what to do, being free to get up and go to bed when they want, being free to walk where they want, and having the opportunity for good clothes, good food, and sex constitute over 80 percent of their responses concerning positive aspects of release. The point here is not that these are unimportant things to look forward to, but that they turn out to be very transient satisfactions. Their predominance in the prerelease period has the potential for creating a disappointing postrelease experience.

Perhaps the most important lesson of this prerelease situation concerns the influence of situational factors in shaping the inmates' attitudes and psychological reactions. In view of the constraints and demands of the prerelease situation, it is difficult to avoid concluding that the most effective, realistic, and adaptive response to this situation is exactly that taken by these boys—to avoid the destructive frustration, impotence, and depression of hardheadedly anticipating the future, and to instead, "think positive." What hope many of these boys will have after release exists precisely in their pulling off a self-fulfilling prophecy of their own.

What is particularly distressing about the failure of the institution to provide even minimal preparation for reentry is that most of these boys seemed motivated to change their lives and to take advantage of any help that might have been offered. All but two of them planned on working soon after release, and none reported any immediate intentions to steal or engage in any other illegal behavior, though about six to eight indicated a willingness to do so if things didn't work out well for them. Only three of the twenty-one former heroin-users expressed any intention to use drugs, though a lot of these boys admitted to doubts about their ability to stay off drugs, especially if other things didn't go well.

One could not help but hear these boys saying that they did not like prison and did not want to have to come back there again. Despite the attraction of heroin use, most of the former users were tired of being junkies. Many boys were at a point in their lives of wanting to settle down and marry their girlfriends. Most seemed to feel that getting out of jail represented a possible turning point in their lives, and most had some desire to do something with it.

Research evidence from studies on prison socialization supports these contentions. A number of studies based on Clemmer's notions of "prisonization" (1940) have attempted to assess the changes an inmate undergoes because of his exposure to "inmate culture." Studies by both Wheeler (1961) and Glaser (1964) found that such changes follow a U-shaped curve. They suggest that there is a maximal identification with the inmate culture (in opposition to conventional values) in the middle of imprisonment, but as release approaches inmates begin to pull away and move much closer to a conventional orientation. Wheeler argues strongly the potential impact of interventions during the release and reentry period. Consistent with the present findings, these studies provide systematic evidence that the reentry period is an important time to help and support inmates' efforts at change.

4 The Forgotten Family

My son was sent to the hospital with a kidney infection and no one ever told me.

Mrs. Jackson

This chapter describes the nature of the interactions the family has with correctional agencies, particularly with respect to the release and return home of their sons. It provides critical data from a second perspective—the experience of the family—for assessing the nature and extent of institutional responsibility for what happens during the reentry period.

Perhaps the best way to understand the essential characteristics of the relationship between the families and the correctional system is through two types of incidents frequently described by the mothers.

1. Fully fifteen of the mothers described the following kind of incident. After being convicted and sentenced, the boy had been incarcerated in the jail in the city where he lived. His mother visited him there, frequently or infrequently as the case may be, during the first couple of weeks of his incarceration. Then came a day for all of these mothers when she went to visit her son, *only to be told that he wasn't there.* When she asked the officer where the boy was, he didn't know—he would have to check. Anywhere from thirty minutes to two hours later the mother was politely told that her son had been transferred to the state reformatory, where all offenders under twenty-one years of age were incarcerated. It was a new policy, she was told, to send all offenders under twenty-one to the reformatory rather than keeping them in local jails. When was he sent? The answer varied, but in a number of cases the boy had been transferred more than one week previously. Why wasn't the mother notified of this transfer? Oh, she would be, was the reply. She should receive an official letter from the reformatory; it was their responsibility to notify families of the transfer. What were the visiting hours and how did she get there? She would have to call the reformatory with those questions—the officer really didn't know. The reformatory could give the best directions. As these mothers recounted the incident, some of the old anger was aroused, but mostly the anger had been replaced by resignation. Many indicated that they really hadn't been that surprised after the initial shock. They had been getting used to such treatment for years.

2. Mrs. Jackson's son had been at the reformatory for a few months when she became concerned because he hadn't written for a couple of weeks. She had

33

found it difficult to visit him, as the reformatory was fifty miles from her home, she had no car, and she worked during visiting hours, which at that time were restricted to weekdays. But she had tried to maintain letter contact with him because she wanted to be sure that he knew she was concerned about him. Now she was worried because he had always answered her letters regularly. She called to find out if he was all right. She was told that he wasn't there, but they didn't know off-hand where he was. She would have to call back in a few hours, after they had had a chance to check. When she called again, she was told that her son had been transferred to the prison hospital at the adult state prison, but that no one at the reformatory knew why. It was Friday afternoon and his counselor had already left. She should call the prison hospital and inquire. Which she did. She was told that he was there and that hospital visiting hours were restricted to weekday afternoons—she should try to come next week. No, she couldn't talk with him on the phone. No, the person didn't know when he had been sent there. No, he didn't know what was wrong. He was just the central switchboard operator. Mrs. Jackson should call back on Monday and speak with someone from the hospital. No, they couldn't tell her before then. When Mrs. Jackson called on Monday, she was told her son was okay but that they didn't give out any more information than that over the phone. She should come visit. Mrs. Jackson managed to get Thursday off to visit her son. Almost a week after she discovered her son was in the hospital, she finally learned that he had been there for two weeks with some kind of kidney infection but was improving and due to return to the reformatory any day. He was a little angry and upset that his mother had not been in contact during his whole stay at the hospital, but Mrs. Jackson was pretty sure that he accepted her explanation. Six mothers said that their sons had received some kind of relatively serious medical attention of which they had not been informed either before or after it happened.

A total of nineteen mothers told of either or both of these kinds of incidents. These examples will be allowed to speak for themselves regarding the nature of the general relationship of families to the correctional system, except to emphasize two aspects particularly relevant to reentry. First is the glimpse they provide into just how deep the sense of exclusion, isolation, and helplessness must be in these families regarding their son's lives while they are in prison. These examples are particularly instructive precisely because they involve especially important events—transfer and illness—and demonstrate that significant things can happen without the families knowledge. The reentry reunion frequently occurs against this background of virtual exclusion from a son's life during a very critical time. Second is the clear indication of just how little regard the correctional system has for even minimal responsibilities to the family relationship needs of both the boys and their parents. As the following data document, even the most elementary needs of the families are seriously neglected.

Information from the Institution:

Other data concerning interaction with the institution flesh out this picture. At the time of their sons' admission to the state reformatory, each family is supposed to be sent a letter indicating that he is there and explaining visiting and letter-writing regulations. Twenty mothers did not remember receiving such a letter. Ten were certain they hadn't; another ten were not certain but did not think they had. However, it is not clear that these mothers were particularly unfortunate in comparison with those who did receive this letter. On the letterhead of all prison stationery, including that used by inmates, visiting hours are stated. Midway through this investigation, visiting privileges were increased from two to four hours per month and visiting hours were extended until seven in the evening. As of the end of the study, the letterhead still had not been altered to reflect this change, and no other notice had been sent out. A handful of mothers indicated that they had continued struggling within the old visiting regulations for a month or more before they finally discovered the change.

Other data indicate that communication with the institutional staff is not and cannot be used as a way to keep in contact with a boy's life in jail. First, there was a very low level of interaction between the families and the institution, and what contact there was rested almost entirely upon the initiative of the family. No one from the reformatory ever visited any of the families. Only twenty mothers had either phone contact with the institution or talked with someone when visiting their sons. Included here are three mothers who indicated they had chatted with guards when visiting their sons, two who had asked for directions to and from the institution, and a few who asked about visiting hours. In only four cases had the reformatory initiated the contact, and this was to inform the mother of the boy's release date.

There is virtually no interaction around issues of the son's welfare, attitudes, change, etc. In fact, the general attitude among the mothers was that it was useless to approach the institutional staff with questions of any kind, let alone questions of this nature. They reported that it was difficult to find anyone knowledgeable and impossible to get them to reveal anything. Twenty mothers reported having some question they wanted to ask about their sons. Eight decided it would be a waste of time to even ask. They were probably right: of the twelve who asked, only three felt they got a satisfactory answer.

One might ask why the mothers didn't have more questions and why they didn't try harder to get information. The examples and data cited should indicate the probable fruitfulness of such attempts. Most of these families were quite aware of the futility of such attempts. Many had had numerous interactions with the criminal justice system in the past and had learned to adopt a very resigned and fatalistic attitude with regard to their son's institutional life. The only real avenue of communication into a son's life in the institution is the son himself. This source is fraught with difficulties (Chapter 10) and also is simply inadequate for many issues.

Bearing in mind that the family is the primary reentry point for the boy and represents his major postrelease resource and source of stability, what kind of preparation do these families receive for their son's return?

Release Date

In the first place, these families do not know much in advance the exact time of their son's return. Though all the families knew the exact release date by the time the interview was conducted (2.5 days before release on the average), in several cases the interviewers arrived only a day or two after the family had been notified. In a couple of cases, the interviewer came very close to providing that notification himself. The average family learned the exact release date only two and a half weeks in advance, and fully sixteen families learned only within the last week before release.

Furthermore, the notification was not typically done by the correctional system itself. Only four families had been notified of their son's exact date by some official from the reformatory. Though a boy's parole officer is supposed to notify the family, only eight of the fourteen families of parolees had been contacted by the time of the interview. All were eventually contacted before release, though in many cases only a day or two before the boy's return. Twenty families had been notified only by their sons. In several cases, the mother indicated that she didn't trust either the accuracy or the honesty of her son's information. Thus, the notification of the families is even later and more uncertain than the notification of the boys.

Even granting that the institution seriously neglects notifying families of release dates, it still seems possible for them to have a better idea of the son's release date than they do—either from their sons or by asking about it. How does this condition arise?

In the first place, it is important to remember that the sentences themselves are generally confusing, involving definite versus indefinite sentences, time off for good behavior, and other factors that affect the actual date. We can safely assume that few families have these complexities explained to them at the time of sentencing. The boy himself may not even fully understand his sentence until he is at the reformatory. At this point communication of the release date rests entirely with the boy. If he experiences as much uncertainty about his date as was noted in the last chapter, he may not want to indicate anything to his family until he is more sure, especially since significant changes are possible right up until the day of release itself. Families' attempts to find out dates are subject to the system's own confusion about the date on the one hand and the significant difficulty of getting information from them on the other. The primary issue is the failure of the correctional system to adequately inform families. In light of the complexity of the system, the possibilities of change, the level of errors made, and the difficulty of getting information, it is difficult to see how the situation could improve much through increased parental efforts alone.

Release Preparation

Of the thirty mothers who planned on driving their sons home, ten had not been told what time of day to pick him up. Of those who had, fourteen had been told by their son only and were frequently very wary of this information. The usual time of release was between 8:30 and 9:00 A.M. Mothers thought this to be very early. Many thought their sons were getting overly enthusiastic and that if they went at that hour they'd end up spending half the day waiting.

Twenty-one of the thirty-two mothers didn't know the conditions of their sons' release, including thirteen of the twenty-five whose sons were to be released on either probation or parole. Twenty of these twenty-five mothers knew nothing of their son's responsibilities under these supervised conditions. In only five cases did the parole or probation officer explain anything to the mother about regulations, usually immediately after release. Thus, there was a very high level of ignorance regarding the nature and regulations of parole and probation. Most families were deprived of even the minimal sense of support that might come from a better understanding and communication with parole and probation officers.

The picture is clear. The family, relied upon by both the boy and correctional agencies as the focal point and major resource of reentry, confronted reentry without forewarning and typically unprepared about even the most elementary aspects of reentry. There was a serious level of ignorance and uncertainty concerning the timing, mechanics, and regulations of release. Most information came from the boys themselves or, in a few cases, from the persistent efforts of the mothers to seek it out. The correctional agencies took virtually no responsibility for providing even a minimal basis for a smooth and productive transition. In this situation it was difficult if not impossible to prepare effectively for a son's return. In many cases, the return of the boy represented a significant crisis for the family, which was good neither for the family nor the boy.

5 Postrelease Overview

This chapter outlines a few of the major postrelease findings in order to provide a context for the detailed descriptions that follow.

Reported Investment of Time

Boys were asked at B2 and B3 to rank four areas—home, girlfriend, street, and job—with respect to where they saw themselves spending most of their time. Figure 5-1 represents the average rank given to each area by the group of boys as a whole.

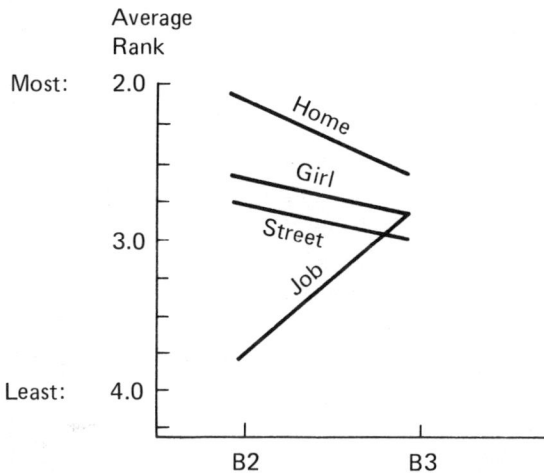

Figure 5-1. Reported Investment of Time: average ranks given at B2 and B3 when asked to rank the four areas of home, girlfriend, street, and job.

The most important finding is the major increase in time spent at work, which reflects the boys' major efforts to secure and maintain employment. The high rank given to time at home and its decline by B3 is also interesting. This high ranking does not necessarily indicate time spent with the family. It in part indicates time spent alone and probably reflects to some extent the alienation of reentry. The decline by B3 again probably reflects mostly their increased work involvement.

Davidson College Library

Friends

Two objective measures reflect what the boys' descriptive reports indicate: these boys spend relatively little time with peers and tend to find relationships with preprison friends either unsatisfactory or unavailable. They were asked to rate on three-point scales the amount of time spent with former (preprison) friends and with all friends (both old and new):

Table 5-1. Mean Ratings on Three-Point Scales (0/1/2) of Time Spent with All Friends (Both) and With Preprison Friends (Former)

		B2	B3	
Both	$\overline{\text{X}}$	.85	1.00	(F = .80, n.s.)
Former	$\overline{\text{X}}$	.85	.54	(F = 4.62, p < .05)

The ratings are relatively low (maximum rating of two), indicating minimal involvement in general, and their ratings of time with former friends decline significantly from B2 to B3, indicating even less involvement in these relationships. These ratings reflect the alienation from peers which is a major part of the reentry experience.

Employment

Prior to release, thirty-two of the thirty-four boys reported that they planned to work soon after release. The postrelease data confirm the sincerity of these intentions. By the end of the first week, fourteen were already either working or due to start a job within a few days. Only six had as yet made no attempt to find a job. By the end of the first month, nineteen were working and four had secured jobs that were to start soon. (Two others were in jail.) All of those still not working had made at least one attempt to get a job and in most cases several attempts. Most jobs were secured through the boys' own efforts and resources. Of the twenty-three jobs secured during the first month out, only two were arranged prior to release by reformatory services, and only two others were procured after release with the help of probation and parole officers. These findings document a serious initial effort to secure and keep jobs.

Residence

By the end of the first week, twenty-eight of the thirty-four boys were living with the families they intended to live with before release, and by the end of the first month only twenty-five were. (Two were in jail.) However, only three boys had moved out because of conflict with their families. The others who had moved were living with relatives and maintained close contact with their families. Overall, 80 percent of the boys had a relatively stable contact with their families. This is not to minimize the substantial difficulties in family relationships that arose during reentry. However, in most cases the difficulties did not immediately endanger the boy's residence with the family. These findings indicate that the family is at least initially available to the boy as an important reentry resource.

Delinquent Involvement

The major illegal activity during reentry is heroin use. (In this study, marijuana use was not considered a delinquent activity.) Of the twenty-one former addicts, fifteen had used heroin at least once by the end of the first month. One used the first day out, eight within the first ten days, and six more within the first month. By the end of the first month, six were using daily, four were using at least twice a week, and five had used once or twice only. Return to heroin use during reentry is clearly rapid and serious.

Outside of heroin use, there was little involvement in delinquent activity, and most is associated with drug use. As of the first week there was only one serious offense (theft). By the end of the first month, two boys were back in jail, and five others had committed serious offenses. However, five of these seven offenses were committed by former addicts (four thefts and one boy selling heroin) and were related to their drug difficulties. In addition to the two in jail, only three others appeared to be getting seriously involved in criminal activities. Hence, outside of actual heroin use and a few drug-related offenses, there is very little delinquent involvement during the first month.

One Year Later

A somewhat cursory check of police and corrections records one year after the interviews were completed showed that seventeen of the thirty-four boys were either back in jail again or sought by the police. This does not include at least four other boys who were already seriously involved with heroin at the close of the study, and our brief record search may well have missed a few boys who had been in and out of jail during that year.

6 The Transition Experience

Coming out cold means a lot of searching for what's happening and what's around.

Bill

This chapter attempts to characterize the processes and experiences during the immediate transitional period, here defined as the first week out. The discussion is based on the interviews conducted with the boys at the end of that first week. Within the sparsely studied reentry area, the issue of immediate transition has been even less closely studied. Yet it is important to do so for a number of reasons.

First, the release and immediate reentry period has already assumed a good deal of significance to the boys themselves prior to release and hence should have an important impact on their feelings and attitudes. Second, this period involves the first real contact with the communities to which these boys are returning, and it is likely that the nature of these contacts will have a lasting influence on subsequent events and experiences. Third, this is a critical point at which to assess the impact of the institutional factors surrounding release. It is quite possible that the direct influence of such factors may fade quickly with increasing distance from the institution, making it critical to examine them at the point of maximum impact. Finally, the immediate transition period may well be critical from the standpoint of interventions. A clear sense of the nature of initial problems, how soon critical events occur, and how significant they are to later adjustments will have important consequences for the timing and nature of interventions.

The B2 interview itself was structured to capitalize on the potential of an interview contact with the boys in the midst of this period. An early part of the interview asked the boys to recount in some detail the main things they had done each day since they got out, referred to later as the *Diary*. A number of questions were asked concerning physical reactions to reentry, perception of and response to changes in people and environment, and emotional responses during this early period of adjustment. Questions were asked about the kinds of positive and negative experiences encountered during this initial week, both in a general sense, and with respect to various specific areas (jobs, friends, family, girlfriends, etc.). It is important to emphasize the advantages of examining these events while they are in progress rather than relying on retrospective reports when the boys memory may well have been affected by intervening events.

Four major findings concerning this transitional period emerged:

1. There is no "honeymoon period." There is immediate struggle and difficulty for virtually all of the boys interviewed. Furthermore, reactions and feelings during transition develop and change very rapidly, a finding that has important implications for the timing of helping interventions.

2. The major characteristics of the transition experience are disorientation, estrangement, and alienation. The corresponding major adjustment task from the boys standpoint is "How do I fit in?"

3. This task represents a major shift from the adjustment task anticipated prior to release, which was basically negative in nature ("How can I avoid trouble and stay out of jail?"). The boys are largely unprepared for this shift in task.

4. The two most important areas of action and concern are jobs and friends. These two areas are most immediately critical to the boys' own definition and assessment of his emerging relationship to the outside world.

Though there are reasonable grounds for hypothesizing at least an initial "honeymoon" period of excitement, the dominant picture is that reentry is unpleasant and difficult. During the interviews themselves, most of the boys appeared quiet and subdued, often confused and frequently anxious. The difficulty of initial reentry was also indicated in response to the opening question: "What has it been like to get out, and what has been happening in the last week?" Twenty-one of the boys responded with essentially negative descriptions of problems, with seven more giving some kind of neutral response, such as "It's been okay." Only six of the responses were clearly positive.

At the same time, it was not immediately clear what the major issues of initial adjustment were. They certainly did not center around unusual or dramatic experiences. In fact, with the exception of the quick heroin use by some boys, one is struck by the ordinariness of the first week as described in the *Diary*. It is pretty much what one would expect from people returning home after a long period away. It is basically a time of reorientation, of seeing family and relatives, of making contact with friends and getting back together with girlfriends, of looking for jobs and starting to work. There is frequent mention of just walking or riding around, either alone or with friends. There is a lot of clothes shopping as the boys seek to get back in style. It is not a time of wild partying and indulgence in pleasures, though there is a little of that. Neither is it usually a week of seclusion at home, though again there are a few exceptions. In general, it does seem to be a week of "searching for what's happening and what's around."

Estrangement

Reentry Shock

Though not immediately visible in discrete events, there is some evidence of just how strong the impact of the reentry experience may be. Some reactions might be termed "reentry shock," or a more or less physical reaction to the changes involved in moving from jail to the outside world.

This reaction is seen most directly in frequent reports of distorted perceptions of both size and time. More than half of the thirty-four boys reported that their homes seemed very small at first. Many also reported having to adjust to how quiet their homes were, to new night sounds (clocks, refrigerators), to the absence of morning wake-up gong, etc. Twenty-four boys experienced time as passing very quickly (six said slowly) in comparison with how slowly it had passed at the reformatory.

There were also a striking number of references to how fast-paced, noisy, and frantic life on the outside seemed and how difficult it was to adjust to, and about a third of the boys described feeling almost overwhelmed when walking down busy city streets. They responded in different ways to the dramatic change in the pace of life. Some seemed frightened and immobilized. Others seemed driven to try to thrust themselves back into the swing of things. Almost two-thirds indicated that they felt they had to be on the move all the time, couldn't sit still, and were anxious when there was nothing to do. More than two-thirds reported difficulties in sleeping.

These data document that reentry does involve a major shift from one physical and temporal environment to a very different one. It is clear that this change has a direct and disconcerting impact on the boys and creates adjustment problems that add to postrelease difficulties.

Feeling "Out of It"

The boys described two major sources of feelings of exclusion and alienation: changes in environments and changes in friends.

They were asked to describe any changes they had noticed in their town and neighborhood and how they had felt about them. Twenty-three of the boys said they had noticed major changes. These changes were of three kinds: (1) downtown renewal: new highways, city buildings, shopping centers, etc.; (2) inner city renewal: a lot of buildings torn down, only sometimes replaced with new apartments; and (3) damage and destruction from summer riots. A typical reaction to downtown renewal was, "It looks nice but it doesn't seem like the same city." Some boys even indicated that they got lost. The strongest reactions, however, were clearly to changes in inner city neighborhoods:

"Everything's been torn down. All the empty lots bother me."

"A lot of buildings are torn down, and the place looks unfit to live in. I don't like the deserted streets."

"All the old hangouts are torn down and the streets are unsafe now, with all the junkies."

In addition to comments like "It makes me feel bad," or "It makes me feel funny and strange," other comments indicate why these changes are troubling:

"All the buildings are torn down. It makes me feel like I missed something because I wasn't here when it happened. It makes me want to know why it happened."

"I can't believe that everything's torn down. I got to get used to it. It would have been different if I had been here when it happened."

These changes were a clear reminder to the boys that *life in the city had gone on without them, and now they felt excluded from it.*

Initial experiences with peers will be discussed in detail shortly. The major initial reaction, however, was that friends had changed, and the boy felt strange with them. More than two-thirds of the boys reported such feelings. The sources of this strangeness ranged from changes in dress styles and slang, to changes in relationships among friends, to changes in the basic composition of the peer group. Initial contacts with peers again made the boy realize that life had gone on during his absence and that he didn't feel a part of it when he returned.

Letdown and Emptiness

A surprising number of boys complained of being bored, of having nothing to do, that nothing was happening. Fully half of the boys complained of this at some point, eight of them reporting this as their primary reaction to release. And this after having left one of the most dull and routinized environments man has created.

In part this finding can be understood in terms of a lack of integration into life patterns that give one a sense of "something to do." They are out of touch with their friends and their activities, and they have not yet reestablished their own routines and daily habits. It may also, however, be a more direct consequence of the prerelease situation. There is strong evidence of a major letdown as a consequence of overanticipating the novelty and excitement of release. This evidence comes from a comparison of responses to questions in all three interviews directed at what they thought was good or positive about getting out. At B1 they were asked what they thought would be good or exciting about getting out and at B2 and B3 they were asked what they had liked best about being out and what had been most exciting about being out. Because of the slight differences in the form of questions between B1 and the other interviews, the data are comparable only on a descriptive basis.

The responses tended to fall into relatively clear categories. "Freedom" includes reponses such as "freedom," "being free," or "being out," as well as "freedom to walk where I want and get up when I want." "Immediate pleasures" include such things as good clothes, good food, booze, listening to music, etc. "Girls and social life" include responses like "girls," "going to bars," "going out on the town," etc. "Steady girl" involved direct references to a stable relationship with one girl. *Nothing* indicates a response of "nothing" to this question. The remaining categories are clear.

The trends become clearer if categories are collapsed. The first three categories are all similar in that they represent pleasures the boys have been deprived of in prison. These three categories represent the most immediate pleasures surrounding release. Second, the categories of work, family and friends can be collapsed with the "other" category, since they show no interesting trends, except their quite low over-all frequencies.[1]

Table 6-1

	Sources of Positive Satisfactions (in Percent)		
	B1	B2	B3
Freedom	78	25	10
Immediate pleasures		15	9
Girls and social life	**6**	14	5
Steady girl		9	26
Work		7	3
Family	8	5	6
Friends		4	4
Other	3	4	7
Nothing	5	17	30
	100	100	100

Table 6-2

	Sources of Positive Satisfactions (in Percent)		
	B1	B2	B3
Immediate satisfactions	84	54	24
Steady girl	–	9	26
Nothing	5	17	30
Other	11	20	20

[1] It is important to note, however, the persistent low significance of work, family, and friends as sources of positive satisfaction during reentry. These areas, in addition to girlfriends (and educational involvement, which was never mentioned), would seem to be particularly crucial cornerstones for successful and stable postrelease adjustment. Yet these boys do not report them as very meaningful and satisfying at all. This is consistent with their more detailed discussions elsewhere of difficulties in these areas. It is indicative of postrelease difficulties that these areas are insignificant enough as satisfactions to warrant their inclusion in the "other" category.

Immediate satisfactions rapidly diminished in significance, with equally large decreases from B1 to B2 and B2 to B3. They still predominate at B2, and they do indeed represent some of the real positive experiences of reentry. The experiences of freedom, of walking out of prison, of eating noninstitutional food, of seeing and being with girls, of wearing real clothes, of sleeping in late—these are pleasurable and important to these boys. Yet they are less predominant in reality than they were in expectation.

The important question then becomes what is replacing them. To a limited extent, they are being replaced by deeper and more stable sources of positive experiences, especially relationships with girlfriends. However, the crucial areas of jobs, friends, and families do not seem to be providing the positive experiences that may be necessary to a stable and meaningful postrelease adjustment.

Most significant is the substantial increase in "nothing" responses, even as early as the first week, when the novelty of release should be highest. By the end of the month if is the most frequent response. This tendency for immediate satisfactions to fade rapidly without being replaced documents a major "let-down," where the excitement and meaning of release simply does not measure up to expectations (which in part have been shaped by institutional prerelease factors noted in Chapter 3). This may be one source of the boredom and depression reported during the first week out. The continuing intensification of this trend during the first month may be even more important. The increasing absence of positive experiences, called here "emptiness," indicates a lack of satisfactions which can compensate for the difficulties these boys are having in critical areas (jobs, family, friends). This will begin to undermine their motivation to continue trying to effect change in these areas.

The discussion so far has attempted to characterize the major aspects of the transitional experience of immediate reentry. Parts of this experience make sense as immediate reactions to release and reentry: reentry shock, strangeness with friends, and feeling "out of it" in changed environments. It is important to note, however, how soon other reactions develop, in particular, boredom and emptiness. One would expect that the novelty and stimulation of release would delay these experiences longer. Their rapid emergence indicates the urgency of the whole reentry process.

We turn now to an examination of the two most critical areas of immediate reentry: friends and jobs.

Friends

Two things predominate in the boys' reports concerning friends: their immediate active attempts to see their friends, and the strong sense of estrangement resulting from these contacts. By the end of the day of release itself, the *Diary* shows that nineteen of the thirty-four boys had seen some of their friends (fifteen by explicitly seeking them out), and by the end of the second day, twenty-eight had seen some friends (twenty-four seeking them out). There was clearly an immediate search to find out who was around and what they were doing. This search is significant only in contrast with the predominant prerelease concern with *avoiding* old friends, when twenty-seven indicated that avoiding at least some previous friends would be critical to succeeding on the outside. At B2, only eleven reported concern with avoiding friends. This active search for friends is not necessarily contradictory with the prerelease intention to avoid friends. Initial contacts do not necessarily constitute attempts to reestablish old relationships. Yet the data document a clear need to establish contact with friends and a definitely reduced concern with avoiding friends.

Most significant is the strong initial sense of estrangement resulting from these contacts. Though almost all reported that their friends seemed glad to see them, more than 75 percent also reported feeling strange or "funny" around them. The predominant theme is that something had changed in their friends that caused the boy to feel out of things.

Dress styles had changed, for example: "Makes me feel out of it and like I have to catch up fast." Slang had frequently changed so that either the boy used out-dated slang or didn't understand what his friends were saying. Relationships among peers had changed and created awkward situations. One boy, used to being the center attraction of his peer group, walked into a party and "left with five enemies." Among other things, he had kidded about a couple only to discover that the relationship had terminated. He left very shaken by the experience.

There were frequently changes in the basic composition of the peer group.[2] Boys returned to find friends missing. Usually they were in jail, sometimes they had moved, and occasionally they had died. "A lot of guys are gone—either in jail or dead." Or there might be new people to contend with. "There's lots of new people on the street, lots of younger guys are taking over—I don't like it." Old companions were not always around, and new people required working out new roles. From a former addict: "All *young* kids are into dope now and taking over—all the ones who used to tell me I was wrong." Even old deviant niches had been taken away.

Finally, the boy might be initially alienated from his friends' activities. If they, for example, were engaged in delinquent activities, he might be afraid to be with them. "They're all junkies now, and into B and E, and I can't hang with them anymore." Or the boy himself might have changed, producing the same result. "Now that I don't use dope, I really feel out of it with my friends." Hence, to the extent that the boy has changed or wants to change, he ends up

---

[2] "Peer group" is used loosely here to mean the collection of all those who were former friends of the releasee, whether they were organized into one group or not. Most frequently they were not.

being alienated from some of his former friends. This is most true for the former addict whose preprison group of friends was more than likely restricted to other addicts only.

At the same time, there is little evidence of direct peer pressures to join delinquent activities. Over-all, delinquent activity during the first week was very low, constituting one theft and some heroin use, and only in two cases of heroin use was it due to pressure from friends.

Release confronted the boys with a major shift in the basic issues concerning friends. Prerelease concerns, though involving some concern with peer changes, basically centered on avoiding friends, on avoiding their influence towards slipping back into old habits, delinquent activities, and jail. The immediate issue at release is not *avoidance*, but the *establishment* of meaningful relationships. They are not confronted with peer influences pressuring them into bad habits or activities that must be avoided. They are confronted with either an absence of relationships or a real discomfort and sense of inadequacy with ones that do exist.

Jobs

Employment may be the most pivotal issue of the whole reentry period. Aged seventeen to twenty-three (average age about twenty), these boys are at a transitional stage in the world of employment. They have long since dropped out of school and have no immediate intentions of returning. Out of school and approaching adulthood, for them a job must be the cornerstone of any successful adjustment. It is expected by probation and parole, by family and community, and in most cases by the boys themselves. Yet they face heavy odds. Skill levels are quite low, employment histories are weak for most, and all come with criminal records. A few even find themselves too young for jobs that would otherwise have been theirs. Most face the necessity of proving the sincerity of their intentions to family and parole officers by working. The significance of jobs to the boys is becoming clear even by the end of the first week out.

The data document an impressive attempt by most to find jobs and start working. Eight of the thirty-four are working already, and six others have jobs that start in a few days. Only six have yet made no attempt to find a job. What makes this even more impressive is that these boys are forced to rely on their own initiatives and resources in getting jobs. Only four of the twenty-three jobs eventually secured during the whole reentry period were arranged by reformatory, probation, and parole services. Indeed, some of the jobs arranged by the vocational rehabilitation counselors failed to materialize because of poor coordination with the regional offices. Most jobs were located through family, relatives, or knocking on employers' doors. In this situation, their active search for jobs is the single most significant indication of the sincerity of most boys' intentions to "make it."

Jobs seem to mean two things to the boys during this first week. First, they are frequently looked to for some kind of structure and direction in the ambiguity of immediate reentry. "Jobs are important because you need something to hang onto when you get out." "You need a job before you know where to start." These comments indicate a need for jobs as an *organizing* element in their lives. Sudden reentry with little preparation has thrust many into a situation where their lives are disorganized and confused, and jobs are a major source of stability.

Jobs are also seen as a critical and necessary sign of their ability to change, stay out of trouble, and make it. This is occasionally seen in comments by those who are working. They frequently say they feel that they are starting off on the right foot. It is more clear from those who are *not* working. Many experience a real urgency to resolve the question of whether or not they will be able to make it, and get upset when they can't find a job immediately. "You really should have a job when you get out because no job means looking, failing, and saying 'fuck it!'" Twelve boys report that failing to secure a job was the major frustration of the first week. They felt at loose ends and concerned that things weren't going to work out right.

Family Relationships

Family relationships are the most positive part of the transition period. It is at B2 that the boys rate their family relationships quite positively, report few concerns, and describe many favorable reactions to their initial family contacts. At the same time, it does appear that both the boy and the family are being cautious and determinedly positive with each other, trying very hard to make things go right. One senses more underlying uncertainties than the boys are willing to talk about, partly because of an unwillingness to question their one and only source of physical and emotional support at release. In a handful of cases there has already been major conflict or a clear indication of rejection by the family. But most boys (80 percent) are pleasantly surprised at how well things are going with their families (details in Chapter 10).

Conclusions

Probably the most important feature of the reentry experience is the task of "fitting in," of finding ways of belonging. This is seen most clearly in peer relationships, where the major need is to establish meaningful relationships, rather than to avoid harmful ones. Fitting in is also reflected in the data on emptiness, and on the meaning of jobs. These boys very quickly confront the need *for* something, not simply the need to *avoid* something. This represents an important shift from prerelease anticipations, when concerns centered on avoiding bad influences—bad friends, dope, and street life. "Avoidance" tasks have by no means disappeared as concerns, but issues of integration, fitting in, and belonging somewhere now predominate. It is a drastic shift for which few of these boys are prepared. It is a task for which the coping response of "keeping a strong mind" seems less adequate.

Jobs already begin to emerge as a critical factor of reentry. Securing a job is seen by the boys themselves as the most important sign of their ability to make it successfully. Frustration and discouragement among those who have failed is already beginning to mount, compounding already substantial doubts about the possibility of change. The boys' considerable motivation and effort to secure jobs remains virtually unsupported by those very agencies that most strongly urge the necessity of employment—parole and probation. It is a cruel contradiction. Providing jobs is perhaps the single most important intervention that could be made during this period.

There are several signs that feelings and reactions change rapidly during reentry. The urgency of reentry processes is seen primarily in the immediacy with which certain reactions emerge, such as boredom, emptiness, and discouragement about the failure to secure a job. The central question is how long real efforts at change will be sustained, for in many cases one can see frustration and discouragement already arising. Some may interpret these reactions in terms of the delinquent's own psychological shortcomings, as reflecting impulsiveness, an inability to delay gratification, a short time perspective. This view ignores the severe pressures and constraints of the reentry situation which underly these reactions, particularly the significant pressure to demonstrate sincere intentions and constructive change quickly despite the absence of preparation and support for a very difficult crisis period.

7
The Fourth Week Out

You've got to think about what you have *to do, not what you* want
to do."

Tony

If the reentry period is defined as that period of time surrounding release
characterized by heightened flux and change in the releasee's life, one can see by
the fourth week out the beginning of the end of initial reentry processes. Most
initial transition problems are disappearing. More important, new problems have
emerged and are already culminating in events that represent potentially critical
turning points in these boys' lives. The resolution of these crises will define
initial adjustment patterns and mark the end of the reentry period. It will be
argued that these processes do delineate a "reentry period" with a discernible
end point—about three to five weeks after release—a period that will most likely
have a lasting influence on these boys' lives.

The discussion in this chapter centers around the third interview with the
boys. The interview had two major purposes: to characterize the problems and
progress of postrelease adjustment at the end of the first month, and to provide,
both through direct questions and through comparisons with B2 data, a picture
of the processes and changes occurring during the first month of release.

It is important at the outset to reemphasize that the reentry experience is an
increasingly negative one. Responses to questions on general reactions to reentry
tend to reflect a higher frequency of negative experiences and little mention of
positive ones. Significant problems are reported in most areas of adjustment,
especially employment and family relationships. Just as there was no peak
positive experience immediately after release, neither is there any immediate
"rebound" from initially negative experiences. Indeed, it seems fair to say that
things start bad and get worse.

At the same time, the reasons for difficulties are changing. Transition issues
of estrangement and alienation seem to be fading substantially, and a new kind
of struggle is emerging. This struggle is well stated in the quote "You've got to
think about what you *have to* do, not what you *wnat to* do." This comment
refers specifically to coping with the sacrifices of working a full-time job, but at
a more general level captures a frequent theme in these boys' descriptions which
indicates a confrontation with some of the realities of their emerging postrelease
lives. (Chapter 5 gives a more complete review of the status of the group at the
end of the first month.)

Work involvement has increased significantly during the first month, and this has brought work issues to even greater prominence than previously. There is substantial uncertainty as to whether significant initial efforts toward working can be maintained, both for those actually working and for those having trouble finding jobs. Heroin use has increased considerably, and many boys are beginning to encounter the problems this involvement creates, particularly at home and at work. Finally, it has been a month of increasing conflict and unhappiness at home, and many boys realize that the changes in family relationships they had hoped for have not happened.

In general, then, the end of the first month seems to be a time of experiencing the consequences of one's initial adjustments, of coming to terms with the nitty-gritty problems of everyday life, and of more actively evaluating one's progress. As one boy put it, "The novelty of being out is over."

The Fading of Transition Issues

Critical changes have occurred with respect to the most prominent characteristics of the initial transition experience, feelings of estrangement and alienation. These seem to be decreasing significantly by the end of the first month. Reports of these feelings are virtually absent in the B3 interviews in responses to questions ranging from specific questions about whether they feel "out of it" (50 percent at B2; 28 percent at B3) and strange with their friends (68 percent at B2; 12 percent at B3) to general, open-ended questions concerning major problems confronted (33 percent at B2; 12 percent at B3). These kinds of feelings are reported as major concerns by no more than four or five boys and simply do not stand out as problems by the end of the first month.

The one transition experience that does persist, and in fact worsens, is that of "emptiness." Throughout reentry, expected and initial sources of satisfaction are losing their meaning and for the most part are not being replaced by other positive experiences (Table 6-2). This absence of positive experiences represents a void many boys are seeking to fill by the most readily available means—heroin use, for example—or which makes it difficult to sustain efforts at those tasks required for successful adjustment—work, for example. Put more directly, there is little that makes it worthwhile for many boys to continue trying to do things differently from the way they used to.

Friends

Initial relationships with friends were a major source of alienation during the first week out, and it is important to see how this problem has been worked out. Though few now report such feelings, the boys seem to have dealt with this problem primarily through minimizing involvement with peers. As a group, they are spending little time with former friends and are not involved in extensive networks of peer relationships. Though their ratings of time spent with all friends (both old and new) do not change from B2, ratings of time spent with their primary preprison friends decrease significantly (means out of a maximum rating of 2). Also, the absolute level of these ratings are less than 1 on a three-point scale, indicating very little over-all involvement.

Table 7-1
Boys Mean Ratings of Time Spent With All Friends ("Both") and With Preprison Friends Only ("Former")

	B2	B3
Both: $\overline{X}$	.85	= 1.00 (F = .80, n.s.)
Former $\overline{X}$	.85	.54 (F = 4.62, p < .05)

Only eight of the boys are heavily involved with a peer *group*, and for only six of them is this group composed of former friends. These are fairly clear indications that most boys find former relationships either unsatisfactory or unavailable.

Very few say that they are intentionally avoiding former friends. Over half say that they "just don't see" their former friends, that they spend their time working, with girlfriends, or with relatives. In part, this reflects their increased involvement with working and with girlfriends. Yet it also sounds like a subtle form of avoidance, either to avoid the risks of association with these friends or because they no longer feel they belong. Overall, the alienating forces described at B2 (changed composition and activities of peer groups, feelings of strangeness, etc.) have made many initial contacts so unsatisfactory that the boys are not significantly involved in them.

At the same time, few are seriously lacking some relationship to satisfy their needs. Only four boys complain of loneliness, of having no friends to spend time with. Most boys have settled down to one or two people who meet recreational and companionship needs, most frequently their girlfriends. About half indicate that they spend most of their free time with their girlfriends. Another handful have reestablished satisfactory relationships with one or two former friends or with relatives close to their own age. The most promising of these relationships are former friends with whom they have never been involved in delinquent activities. The boys see these relationships as indicating a positive break with the past. Their activities with these friends are not felt to be repetitions of old patterns leading to the same problems and are seen instead as positive signs of "making it."

To a certain extent, these patterns reflect positive developments. The boys are breaking away from prior trouble-prone relationships and establishing new, more productive ones. That this is occurring for many is clear, yet the picture at this point may be masking some potential problems. First, direct concern with peer relationships may be overshadowed by struggles with jobs and drugs, which are more immediate critical signs of making it. For example, the lack of more friends outside of girlfriends may come to be of more concern as these other issues resolve themselves, particularly the absence of peer relationships that support attempts to work full time. As will be seen, maintaining full-time work can be very difficult without friends who experience the same sacrifices. Second, some former addicts seem to have resolved initial estrangement from friends by using heroin with them. This quickly reestablishes relationships but on a basis that offers little hope for the future.

Yet, on the whole, friends are not a major problem at this point, particularly in comparison with other areas.

Girlfriends

Relationships with girlfriends play an important role in the reentry period. They are a major source of positive experiences, a predominant source of companionship and support for many, and frequently provide a real focus of stability during this period.

Two-thirds of the boys report a satisfying relationship with a girlfriend. About half of these are continuations of preprison relationships and about half are with new girlfriends, though usually with girls known previously. As shown in the analysis of positive experiences, girlfriends are the primary source of positive experiences by the end of the first month. In the initial context of strange and uncomfortable contacts with male friends, many turn to girls for companionship and end up spending a good deal of their free time with them.

Girlfriends have some unique advantages as a source of support, encouragement, and stability. Unless the girl has been associated with past drug use, involvement with her does not seem to threaten a return to "old habits" as readily as involvement with former male friends does. Neither is the relationship tied up with the mutual ambivalence and conflict that frequently interferes with the family's ability to fill this role. In the best cases, a girlfriend can provide both encouragement and an outlet for desires to settle down and stay out of trouble.

The Turning Point of Reentry

By far the most significant finding of the last interviews is the indication that a major turning point in postrelease adjustment occurs somewhere around a month after release. A number of reentry pressures are culminating in critical events. Their resolution will define initial adjustment patterns and probably have a decisive effect on the boys' motivations to "make it."

The underlying issue is revealed most directly in the boys' typical responses to the final interview question about what other boys should be prepared to face when they get out:

"You've got to think about what you *have* to do, not what you *want* to do."

"You have to make yourself do what you *have* to do."

"You have to learn to face responsibilities."

"You have to realize that if you don't straighten out, you'll end up in 'S' (an adult state prison)."

These comments indicate that at this time many boys are confronting the realities of life on the outside. Whether this involves sacrifices entailed in full-time work or the recognition that one is becoming a junkie again, these boys are beginning to come up against some of the longer-range consequences of their initial life styles. This issue, and the critical events it precipitates, center primarily around families, drug use, and especially jobs.

With respect to jobs, those working are finding it very difficult to deal with the sacrifices of full-time work and the extensive impact working has on the rest of their lives. Very few like their jobs, most find them difficult, and several are thinking of quitting. For those who have not yet secured a job, frustration and discouragement are extremely high. Most take their failure as a sign of their own inability to "make it" and are close to abandoning serious efforts.

The same kind of issue is also reflected in an increased willingness to admit concern about drug use. At B2 there was a surprising lack of concern, with twelve out of the twenty-one ex-addicts saying that drugs were no problem for them, including four of the six who had already used drugs. By B3, however, only five of the twenty-one now claim that drugs are no problem, and twelve of the fifteen who have now used admit that it is a major problem. Most of those using heroin are openly worried about becoming junkies again, or at least about the consequences at home and work of continued use.

Problems in family relationships also reflect the same issue. Their general descriptions clearly indicate substantially more unhappiness and disappointment than before. For some this means a return to a more typical problematic plane in their relationships. For others it involves the emergence of significant conflict. In general, far fewer hopes for change are now verbalized. Initial optimism has disappeared, and the long term reality of problems is setting in. Close to 25 percent of the boys have left or about to leave home because of problems with their families.

At a more nitty-gritty level, those not working are now experiencing the crunch of not having enough money. Whereas at B2 only two report money as a major problem, eleven do at B3. Neither they nor their families are happy with the boy using scarce family resources for pocket money, and moreover, they are usually in agreement that the boy should be contributing rent money. One boy has already stolen, and four others are considering theft or dealing drugs if jobs don't come through soon.

So, in one form or another, a lot of the difficulties described involve a confrontation with the consequences of initial life styles. There are two aspects to this confrontation. At a concrete level, a number of difficult problems are coming to a head at this time: lack of money, drug problems, work sacrifices, family conflict, etc. Yet what turns this into a real crisis is the projection of these difficulties into the future. It is the anticipation of *continued* work sacrifices and family conflict that is difficult to come to terms with; it is the expectation of *continued* failure at finding jobs and earning money that is difficult to tolerate; it is the glimpse that one is again headed down the road to being a junkie that is frightening. For many of these boys it is a time of "taking stock" of where they are and where they are likely to go. How they decide to relate to the particular crises at work, at home, and with drugs will determine the next direction their lives will take.

Jobs

Jobs continue to be the most significant problem area during reentry, both for those who have jobs and those who don't. Significant efforts to secure and maintain employment have continued throughout the first month. Nineteen are now working (versus eight at B2), and four others have jobs that start soon (versus six at B2). Everyone by now has made at least one attempt to get a job, with most having showed persistent attempts. The basic question at this point is whether this effort will be maintained.

The boys have the expected kinds of jobs—low-paying, unskilled manual labor, ranging from garbage collection and building maintenance to work in factories and unskilled work in printing shops. Many of the jobs are strenuous, most are unrewarding, and very few have any real future. The only really promising jobs are with relatives who have their own businesses. The best is as a carpenter's apprentice with the boy's father. Very few like their particular jobs (only four of the nineteen who are working), and seven are already considering either quitting or looking for other jobs. Their dislike of working very clearly reflects the nature of their jobs.

Equally significant, however, is the difficulty they face in adjusting to the sacrifices entailed in working full time. More than half report this as a major problem. What becomes clear is the extent to which full-time work involves major changes in life style for these boys, certainly in comparison with their lives in prison, where work demands were minimal, and usually in comparison with their preprison lives, when very few were steady workers.

They quickly confront the amount of energy full-time work takes. They come home so tired in the evening that they can't do much but sleep. They also begin to realize just how much full-time work cuts into their free time, both directly in terms of hours spent at work and indirectly in terms of subsequent fatigue. They also begin to realize what it means to work at a monotonous job day after day and to project that monotony into the future. These sacrifices may be particularly difficult to endure immediately following release from prison, when there is an understandable desire to relax and take it easy for a while. In addition, very few have working friends. The problem is not that nonworking friends downgrade working; it is simply that their lives are not also organized around working; they don't live by the same schedules or experience the same sacrifices, and are not in a position to support work efforts. Indeed, the releasee's working tends to interfere with relationships with nonworking peers. All of these pressures are coming to a head by the end of the first month. About half of those working are adjusting reasonably well, but for the other half there seems to be a serious question of whether the payoffs of working outweigh the sacrifices. It is not an easy question.

Those not yet working face possibly even greater frustrations. None of these boys are at all happy about not working, and all but two have made numerous and consistent attempts to secure jobs. They are almost uniformly frustrated and discouraged by their failure to begin work. In addition to seeing this failure as a sign of their inability to "make it," not working also places the boy in a very uncertain and tenuous situation during reentry. He tends to see working as crucial to avoiding behavior patterns that have gotten him into trouble in the past. Yet without a job he finds himself in the position of avoiding familiar activities and relationships while having little to replace them with. It places him in a kind of limbo that apparently has to be resolved soon—one way or another.

Somewhat surprisingly, there is very little indication that the boy's criminal record has anything to do with his difficulty in securing jobs. At least the boys report virtually no discrimination, despite this being a potentially easy and acceptable rationalization for their own difficulties. Though not explored in detail, more significant factors seem to be low skill levels, lack of experience, age, and the simple unavailability of jobs.

Jobs seem to be the critical factor in whether the releasee fits in new or old ways. The boys themselves see jobs as crucial to change. Failure to find jobs leaves few alternatives to old patterns and creates self-doubts about one's ability to change. Full-time work entails major sacrifices and changes in life style, and it is here that the absence of positive satisfactions, described as "emptiness," seems most significant. The absence of compensatory rewards and satisfactions creates in many ways a legitimate question as to whether it's all worth it or not.

Summary and Conclusions

Somewhere between three and five weeks after release is the turning point of reentry. It is marked by a number of crises whose resolution will define initial adjustment patterns and determine the next direction of the boy's life. It is helpful to summarize more systematically the nature and extent of those crises. Only eight of the thirty-four boys are clearly free of any turning-point crises, and many are experiencing several.

1. Ten of those working indicated the difficulty of sticking with a full-time job and three openly admit thoughts of leaving it.

2. The frustration of being unable to secure a job is especially critical for four boys. One has just given up looking further, and two others are about to.

3. One-third of initial heroin use occurs during this period.

4. The consequences of earlier heroin use are creating critical problems for seven boys by jeopardizing their jobs and threatening their family relationships.

5. The money pinch is getting bad. Two boys have stolen, and four others are ready to steal or to deal drugs.

6. Two boys left home after the third week because of conflict with families, and about five others are close to doing so.

It seems warranted to consider these as turning-point crises. Quitting a job or giving up looking for one, returning to heroin use or criminal activity, and leaving home precipitously all involve important changes in life situations which will certainly influence subsequent adjustments.

The real significance of these events is that they represent a turning point in the boys' belief in the possibility and meaningfulness of change. They are confronting the basic question of whether to keep trying or to give up. For those who are working, the question is whether it is worthwhile to *maintain* the changes they have achieved. For those trying to find a job the question is whether it is worthwhile to continue trying to *initiate* change. And for a number of drug-users, the question is whether they should continue to *hope for* change. The implication is not that they will immediately turn to a life of crime if they give up. Many are simply ready to abandon active efforts to direct their lives in positive ways and to adopt a more fatalistic attitude of letting whatever happens, happen. It is this underlying issue that is coming to a head by the end of the first month. These crises are also threatening the few potential sources of support and stability in these boys' lives, most importantly jobs and family residence. The loss of these critical supports may well make renewed efforts at change much more difficult.

8 The Meaning of Reentry

Maybe I'm just not the kind of person who can ever make it.
Frank

This chapter assesses the importance of the reentry period. It focuses primarily on two major issues. First, it attempts to crystallize more clearly what these boys are telling us about what reentry means to them and the impact it is having on their lives. Second, it assesses the relative significance of the reentry period in the context of the larger social realities to which these boys are returning. Of particular importance is the question of whether the impact of reentry itself is at all significant when contrasted with the general community forces at work in the disadvantaged communities in which these boys live.

Reentry and Personal Change

Though it may appear to restate the obvious, the central concern to the boys during reentry is how to "fit in," how to establish some sense of belonging and integration with the outside world. The particular struggles of doing this have been described in some detail. These difficulties arise in virtually all areas of the boy's life—with friends, with family, with finding and holding jobs, etc. In part these difficulties have been imposed by the isolation of imprisonment. People and communities have changed in the boy's absence, and old roles, activities, relationships, and ways of fitting in are simply not immediately available. These difficulties are compounded by the disorientation of moving from an institutional prison environment to very different outside environments.

More important, however, the significance of the concern with how to fit in is intensified by the fairly serious desires most boys have of fitting in in new ways, of effecting *changed* relationships with the outside world. Most have strong desires, at least initially, to make it. They do not like prison; they are tired of being junkies; they do not like the pain they have caused their families; and to a significant extent, they would like to settle down and lead more acceptable lives. It is the question of how they will fit in, and in particular, whether they will continue to attempt to do so in new and different ways, that is being decided at the end of the reentry period.

What is particularly important to understand is that to some extent, reentry represents to these boys an *opportunity* to change. Most boys perceive reentry as

61

a chance to start anew (*"This time* I'm going to make it!"). In part, this perception comes from the break with previous patterns of roles and activities which imprisonment has imposed and which seems to suggest to them some possibility of change. In part, it is shaped by society's admonition that return to the community is their chance to demonstrate change ("You have done your time; now is your chance to show that you can straighten out"). Though there is considerable variation in the extent to which the boys really trust this perception, it is an issue with which all of them must come to terms, whether that means trying hard to make use of the opportunity, or doubting and avoiding it. Despite this underlying ambivalence, most boys do seem to enter this period with relatively strong intentions of trying to take advantage of the opportunity they think it represents.

Yet we see just how rapidly the boys seem to be abandoning these efforts at change. Despite initial serious efforts, some have already given up, and many others are about to. The reentry period is clearly decisive to the boy's motivation to change, and the critical question becomes why quitting occurs so quickly. The changes involved are difficult and extensive, requiring far more than a month to achieve and involving as many short-term failures as successes. Why do they start to give up so soon?

Part of the difficulty of sustaining efforts at change stems from the institutional and situational factors surrounding release and reentry: the abruptness with which the problems are confronted; the absence of any prerelease planning or preparation; the disorientation created by the environmental transition from institution to community; the pressure from families, in part shaped by the institutional forces, to demonstrate success quickly; and perhaps most important, a prerelease situation that has created exaggerated "either/or" expectations of postrelease alternatives (either I make it quickly or I end up back in jail) and thus has heightened overreactions to short-term frustrations and failures. These situational constraints create an almost impossible task of adjustment. The changes these boys seek simply cannot be achieved as quickly as they feel they must. If these situational pressures could be minimized, efforts at change could be sustained longer.

It is also necessary to examine this issue in terms of what change means to these boys. First, one must appreciate just how potentially extensive the implications of change are in their lives. The notion of "life style," meaning a set of activities, attitudes, and relationships that integrate the individual with his social environment, is helpful to understanding the implications of trying to "fit in" the outside world in new and different ways. The changes required tend to touch all areas of their lives. Furthermore, the various spheres of their lives are interrelated and interdependent, such that change in one sphere will tend to affect the others. Perhaps the best examples are the changes in peer relationships, recreational patterns, self-attitudes, and family tolerance of short-term job difficulties which will be required to support efforts at full-time work. The changes sought tend to require adjustments in the boy's basic life style and hence are difficult and pervasive.

Second, the major issue of change during reentry is the search *for* something—for jobs, new relationships with friends and family, supporting satisfactions. Seeing the immediate adjustment issues primarily in terms of the avoidance of negative influences, as parole tends to do, misses the fact that during reentry at least, what is needed is not so much the prevention of anything as the availability of alternatives. The scarcity of viable, *supported* alternatives makes sustaining efforts at change difficult.

Third, *change means giving up something.* It may mean giving up some friends, some free time, some sources of excitement and satisfaction, or some freedom from responsibility. The question of what makes these sacrifices worthwhile becomes crucial. Again, this is most clear among those working. They have achieved enough change to experience the sacrifices but have not yet evolved a supporting life style to make these sacrifices worthwhile. The absence of compensating satisfaction indicated in the "emptiness" analysis indicates that the payoff of sustaining efforts at change will be a critical, and certainly legitimate, issue. The question of what makes it all worthwhile cannot be thought of solely in terms of the value of lives that keep them out of jail.

Finally, the *process* of change intensifies the ambiguity and uncertainty of reentry. In addition to the initial unavailability of previous social identities, the attempt to change involves struggling toward unfamiliar life styles. These boys were, for example, largely unfamiliar with both the demands and payoffs of lives that center around full-time employment. They were in the dilemma of resisting old roles and activities, which would provide a sense of social integration, without having any clear and understandable replacements. One cannot tolerate such a state of "transition" for long. By the end of the reentry period, these boys had to know how they were going to fit in. Since old roles and activities were clearer and more available than new ones, many were abandoning significant efforts at change for more familiar relationships to society.

Most fundamentally, however, they were giving up on change because they confronted the reality of an essentially closed opportunity structure. Jobs were difficult or impossible to get and provided little future or satisfaction; there were few alternatives for companionship and recreation to those used previously; there were few alternatives for dealing with family conflict other than leaving home; the absence of supportive and helping relationships provided little sense that anyone else thought the boy could or should make it. Hence, to a large extent they were giving up because their perception of reentry as a real opportunity was exposed for what it essentially is—a myth with little support in reality.

This last point will undoubtedly be countered with the argument that it denies the important role that the psychological limitations of the offender play in his giving up on change. This argument tends to run that change is of course difficult, and that work is unsatisfying for a lot of law-abiding people, too. What one confronts, it continues, are the boys' lack of control over immediate impulses and inabilities to delay gratification and to work for future goals. These personal limitations are critical in deciding whether the boys take advantage of the reentry opportunities that do exist; indeed, they must learn "to do what they *have* to do, not what they *want* to do." Unless they can learn to take responsibility for their own behavior, they will continue to fail to take advantage of even better opportunities that might be provided.

There is perhaps enough truth to this argument to make it a tempting one. However, as a *general* explanation of reentry failure, it severely risks "blaming the victim." For example, it ignores the bleakness the future holds for most of these boys, a future that raises serious question as to whether it is in fact worth making sacrifices or delaying gratifications for. Neither does it give enough recognition to the significant efforts these boys have made during reentry and the serious absence of support provided them in these efforts. Without denying the substantial personal difficulties many would have in effecting real change in their lives, it is nevertheless clear that reentry is a situation in which even the most motivated and hard-working individual would have difficulty in trying for very long.

The difference in these positions ultimately boils down in large part to a political one. They differ in the assumptions made concerning how responsive the opportunity structure is to ex-offenders, the kinds of aspirations it is reasonable for ex-offenders to hold, and where the relative balance of power and responsibility lies for opening up real opportunities—within the individual or within social institutions. If one assumes a responsive opportunity structure to exist for those motivated and capable of working to take advantage of it, then it is quite reasonable to identify significant responsibility for postrelease failure in the personal limitations of individuals. If, however, one believes the opportunity structure to be essentially closed and unresponsive, and the individual offender to have little power to influence it, then psychological limitations become largely irrelevant to understanding the major sources of reentry quitting and failure. This essentially political difference in perspective will assume major importance in the final chapter concerning alternative intervention approaches to reentry. For present purposes, it should be said that it was clear in the current research that reasonable and supported opportunities did not exist for most boys and that a variety of situational factors conspired to severely limit the individual's capacity to develop them himself.

The Lasting Impact of Reentry

These issues highlight the question of the long-term significance of the reentry experience on these boy's lives, particularly in contrast with the forces at work in the disadvantaged communities to which they are returning (e.g., the limited resources and opportunities in poor communities and the stresses of poverty on individual and family). If the major reasons for reentry failure do indeed reside in an essentially closed and unresponsive opportunity structure, then what lasting significance can the reentry experience itself, however difficult it might be, have in the context of this larger social reality? Though the absence of longer follow-up with these boys makes any answers speculative, the question needs to be addressed, particularly in assessing the importance of interventions during this period.

Clearly, the kinds of postrelease adjustments made will in the long run depend fundamentally on the kinds of opportunities available to these boys. If meaningful opportunities for productive adjustments are not available, then satisfactory adjustments obviously cannot occur. Though this and most other reentry studies indicate that reentry is managed in ways that make it difficult (if not impossible) to take advantage of those limited opportunities that do exist, in the long run the responsiveness of social and community institutions to the needs and aspirations of the releasee will determine his fate more than the reentry experience itself. It is these institutions which control the resources necessary for productive adjustments. This perspective serves to place the reentry experience in a more realistic context. It suggests that the basic problems confronting released offenders are not particularly unique or special. It can be argued, for example, that these boys are struggling with the same stresses of poverty, the same limited opportunities, and the same class and racial oppression that shape the lives of all boys, delinquent or not, who live in disadvantaged communities. Ultimately it is these issues which must be confronted if we are to expect released offenders to establish meaningful community lives.

Yet this larger social reality should not be allowed to obscure the significance the reentry experience itself seems to have on the individuals who go through it. The kinds of immediate impacts it has suggest that its effects will extend beyond the reentry period in ways that will hasten the process of social failure, provoke further involvement in delinquent life styles, and reduce responsiveness to any subsequent opportunities for change. The effects of reentry suggest that this is a critical time to help the individual address the larger social realities discussed above.

The major immediate impact of reentry is on the boy's belief in the possibility of change. However fleeting or illusory, reentry was perceived as an opportunity for change. Significant efforts by most to effect change were met mostly with frustration and frequently with failure. The significance of the reentry experience is that it tends to convince the boy that change is *not* possible and, moreover, that no one else really believes in or cares about his changing. Furthermore, the boys appear to personalize the reasons for their failure: "I'm just not the kind of person who can make it." The reentry experience seems to intensify feelings of social isolation and personal expendability. Perhaps most basic, it leads the boy to feel that he qualifies only for a marginal and delinquent status in society.

One would expect these impacts to have important effects beyond the reentry period itself. If an individual has been convinced that change is unlikely or even impossible, and unwanted by others as well, then he is much less likely to attempt change in the future. He will be more ready to drift even further into those marginal and delinquent roles for which he perceives himself qualified. To the extent that his destiny will be determined by his own attitudes, motivation, and world view, the reentry experience is likely to exercise an important lasting influence.

The consequences of the reentry experience may be particularly intense for the youthful offender (ages sixteen to twenty-one) because of his transitional status both within the criminal justice system and in the outside community. Legally he is treated neither as a juvenile nor yet as fully an adult offender. There tends to be more flexibility in his sentencing than for adults, and he is usually incarcerated in a reformatory rather than an adult prison. However, subsequent criminal violations will soon lead to sentencing and incarceration as a full adult, with longer imprisonment and more difficult institutional life. Hence, if the discouragement of reentry causes him to drift further into delinquent activities, it will precipitate a major shift in the nature and the intensity of his involvement in the criminal justice system.

The youthful offender is also in a transition stage with respect to his social and community status—from youth to adult roles and expectations. This is true with respect to many spheres of his community life, including education, employment, peer relationships, girlfriends, and family status. His community and family are beginning to expect him to establish himself as an independent and responsible adult. The boys in this study were aware of and sensitive to these expectations, and most wanted to make this change. Reentry failure experiences that convince them of the impossibility of making these changes, at a point when they are particularly concerned with doing so, may have especially lasting effects on their future aspirations and efforts at change.

Overall, these various observations do argue strongly that the reentry experience itself is likely to have some important long-term influence on the lives of released offenders, particularly because of the effects it has on their motivation and self-attitudes. They emphasize the importance of providing effective help to releasees during reentry. Yet if this help is to address the most fundamental problems of reentry it must recognize that the eventual adjustments made will be determined less by the attitudes and motivation of the releasee than by the availability of meaningful opportunities and by the responsiveness of social institutions to his needs and aspirations. In this sense, "reentry," the transition from prison to community, is not really the central problem. The reentry period simply represents a particularly important time to address the more fundamental task of reintegration, which implies, as the "reintegration model" clearly specifies (see Chapter 1), that as much effort must be directed at changing social institutions as at influencing the attitudes and behavior of the individual offender.

This discussion of the impact of reentry on releasees, and of the ultimate responsibility of community institutions for reintegration, must not be allowed to hide the specific responsibility of correctional agencies for the immediate problems of reentry. The critical issue of reentry itself is not so much the offender's needs and problems during this period as it is the negligence of those correctional agencies—the institution, the department of correction, probation and parole—responsible for meeting these needs. These agencies both create many reentry problems and take little responsibility for helping the releasee manage reentry. We have seen in some detail how a variety of institutional factors create both pre- and post-release problems for the releasee. We have also seen how these various agencies fail to prepare either the boy or the family for release, do not ensure the transfer from one agency to another, do not provide supportive services during the transition period, and do little to help secure meaningful jobs or educational opportunities. It is not unfair to say that they do nothing regarding even the most elementary needs of reentry except to make them worse. If this particular correctional system is at all typical—and there is little reason to assume that it is not—then it is clear that unless this negligence is faced squarely as the major issue of reentry, there is little hope that correctional practice will ever effectively address the more fundamental task of reintegration. This issue is the focus of the final chapter.

In conclusion, it is important to discuss the implication of this research for the concepts of labeling and stigma, currently important in theories of criminal careers. Some writers (e.g., Wheeler and Cottrell 1969) suggest that institutionalization furthers the process of isolating social deviants by branding them with stigmatized labels (offender, ex-offender, convict, ex-convict). These labels and the stigma attached to them then persist and determine the attitudes and behavior of both the individual and others around him in ways that seriously interfere with his reintegration into society, thereby intensifying his deviant status.

The present findings suggest that the importance of stigma may be overrated, at least during the reentry period. The boys were asked specifically, regarding a number of adjustment areas, whether having been in prison contributed to their difficulties. Despite the fact that claiming discrimination on the basis of their records would offer a convenient rationalization for a whole range of difficulties, it was virtually never mentioned. Indeed, it appeared that in the communities where these boys lived it was no big deal to have spent some time in the "joint." It was not at all unusual and was even somewhat expected.

This suggests that the reentry experience itself may be of greater significance than stigma in fostering an increasingly deviant and alienated relationship to society. Postrelease failure experiences and the absence opportunities and support appear much more significant in destroying efforts at conventional adjustments than the stigma of being an ex-convict. These boys do not seem to be saying, "People see me as just a criminal" or "I'm afraid to admit I've done some time in prison." Rather they seem to be saying, "I tried and I don't fit in" or "I'm just not cut out for working" or "Nothing has changed—I'm just never going to make it." Undue emphasis on attributing reentry problems to labeling and stigma, which assigns major responsibility to the effect of institutionalization, risks disguising the significant failure to provide real opportunities and real support for conventional adjustments.

Moreover, it is possible that the reentry experience may have a more important impact on the offender's life than the time he spends in the institution. During reentry he confronts quite directly the nature and possibilities of his relationship to his community. Because reentry is seen as an opportunity to change this relationship, his own personal failure and the lack of support he receives from others may do more to further his sense of alienation than does the much longer isolation of imprisonment.

9 Heroin Relapse During Reentry

*At first, it felt funny being with my friends, but when I "got off,"
everything was the same as always.*

Johnny

Any discussion of heroin use during reentry must begin with the distressingly
rapid return to use. Twenty-one of the thirty-four boys in this study had been
addicted prior to incarceration. Of these twenty-one, fifteen had already used
heroin by the end of the first month after release. Nine of these had used within
the first ten days out. By the end of the first month, six were using daily, and
four others were using at least twice a week. In only three cases did successful
abstinence look at all likely.

This exceedingly quick return to serious heroin involvement is particularly
distressing in light of a genuine prerelease desire in most cases not to become
involved with heroin again. Clearly, the major task of the following analysis must
be an attempt to explain this rapid failure to follow through on intentions.
Hence, the primary focus is to assess reentry pressures towards relapse.

This chapter is based on all three interviews with the twenty-one former
addicts. It pertains only to heroin use. Though there was substantial marijuana
use and some use of LSD and amphetamines, neither was widespread nor
significant enough during reentry to warrant special focus.

Characteristics of the Drug Group

Of the twenty-one former addicts, twelve were white and nine were black. Their
average length of incarceration (7.62 months) and their average age (twenty)
were not different from the nonaddicts.

The severity of prior addiction is difficult to assess. The quality of heroin
varies from city to city and time to time, making a "bags per day" measure
unreliable. Also, the extent of any individual's heroin use varies considerably
over time, depending on his ability to buy and various factors in the boy's life
which affect his use. However, even with these limitations, the data indicate that
all twenty-one boys were significantly addicted prior to incarceration. The
average use claimed was eleven bags per day, which represented a habit of
between $70 and $110 per day, depending on the local price. Reported habits
ranged from as low as two or three bags per day to claims of more than twenty.

69

Almost as many boys with lower rates of use described themselves as being seriously addicted as did those with higher rates. The average number of years of addiction was two and a half, ranging from one to seven years. All of the boys indicated that drug use had created serious problems for them, and none romanticized their past drug use.

The reformatory had offered them virtually nothing in terms of counseling or treatment. One of the counselors had run trial drug-counseling groups in which two had been involved. None of the others had received any help. To them, the reformatory simply represented a period of time when they were not "strung out." Many said that it was the longest period they had been off heroin in years, and that they felt good about recovering their health, weight, and general appearance.[1] Though drugs were sometimes available in the reformatory, none of these boys indicated that they had used any heroin in prison.[2]

Prerelease Expectations

Prior to release virtually all these boys said they did not want to become junkies again. Only three of the twenty-one admitted any intention of using heroin, including only one who said he definitely would. About a third did say they would like to use heroin if they could do so without getting hooked, but that they knew they couldn't. Basically, none of these boys liked being a junkie. They were tired of the continual hassle to get drugs, of the deterioration of their health and appearance, of being involved in theft and getting busted, and of the pain they had caused their families.

However, they were generally very unsure about whether they would be able to stay off drugs. Two-thirds of them anticipated at least some difficulty in abstaining, and the following was a typical comment: "I don't want to and I don't plan to, but I don't know what it's like out there and I don't know how I'll feel out there."

Though this may in part reflect hedging on a real commitment to abstain, it is a fundamentally realistic response. Not only had these boys had no help in thinking through the approaching problems and temptations, they had had no opportunity to experience and test out their reactions to the situation they would confront at release. They simply had no way of knowing how well changes in feelings and motivations would hold up when they returned to the real problems in the streets.

---

[1] Their parents frequently commented on these changes as the most visible signs of progress in their sons. The boys seemed like "their sons" again.

[2] Apparently heroin use in the reformatory was at a relatively low level during the period of this study in early 1970. Discussions with counselors, guards, and inmates not in the study failed to reveal any significant heroin use in the reformatory.

Postrelease Findings

The variability in the boys' difficulties with abstaining, in the reasons underlying their initial use, and in their reactions to that use needs to be emphasized at the outset. Conditioned as we are by a public media which tends to portray "drug use as drug use" wherever and whenever it is found, and heroin as an all-powerful drug that seizes control of the individual regardless of personality and circumstance, we tend to expect a good deal of similarity in the problems experienced by users. But there are striking individual differences. This caution is particularly important in view of the immediacy of relapse for many, which risks confirming the uniformity one expects to find.

For example, abstinence was not a struggle at all for some boys, despite their being subject to essentially the same pressures and circumstances as those who used. Three or four of the six who successfully abstained genuinely seemed to have experienced no difficulty in doing so. Nor did the ease or difficulty of abstaining seem related to the extent of past drug use. Finally, there was simply wide variability in the circumstances that provoked initial postrelease drug use.

Most of the observed variability centered on when initial use occurred after release. Hence, after describing a few general characteristics of the reentry period relevant to heroin use, the bulk of the discussion will examine the pressures towards relapse at different points in the reentry period.

General Characteristics of the Reentry Situation

As one would expect, heroin was readily accessible after release, and these boys were immediately confronted with the temptation to use. Seventeen of the twenty-one boys had already been in a situation of possible heroin use within the first week after release. Though two boys explicitly sought it out, and two others were sought out by friends who were pushers,[3] the others simply came into contact with an acquaintance who offered them some heroin. Furthermore, the initial confrontation with heroin usually occurred in a context that made use very easy. The heroin was typically offered by a friend or relative, it was offered free and in a friendly way, and the immediate risks were very low. Finally, the initial exposure frequently came from long-standing relationships—friends, girlfriends, even relatives—making it a very difficult situation to avoid. Two boys returned to girlfriends who were using, and two others had a sister at home who used. Although it is possible that many boys intentionally sought out opportunities, most would practically have had to isolate themselves at home to avoid exposure entirely.

[3] In only two cases was there any problem with heroin being actively "pushed" on the boys. The initial postrelease exposure was much more informal than that.

Though the opportunity to use heroin was immediately available, help in dealing with drug problems was not. Only one boy was in a drug program (nonresidential), and two others were involved in weekly drug groups with their probation officers. The only other "help" available was the parole or probation stipulation that the boys report weekly to a clinic for a urine check. Parole and probation officers themselves typically did no more than warn or threaten the boys about heroin use.

These boys were clearly struggling with these problems alone, with no help from anyone except their parents. Parental attempts at help or control were usually perceived by the boys as nagging or as signs of distrust, and only worsened the struggle. If one views this situation in terms of the strength of competing influences, opportunity and temptation clearly predominated.

Finally, the reentry period was more stressful for former addicts than for others. The intercorrelation analysis contrasts former addicts with nonaddicts on all measures. Although few differences between the groups are indicated, differences that do exist are in the direction of greater difficulty and more stress for the former addicts (Appendix).[4]

Prior to release former addicts more frequently said that short time was hard and reported more depression, though there were no differences on other important measures (excitement, expectancy for success, etc.). At B2 there was a significant tendency for the former addicts to rate emotional reactions more negatively and to report more physical symptoms. There were no significant differences in feelings of strangeness, involvement with peers, or family problems. The measures at B3 begin to reflect the consequences of increasing drug use itself. There was a significant tendency for former addicts to rate over-all progress more negatively, to rate reentry as more difficult, to report more feelings of strangeness, and to indicate greater family conflicts. These data suggest that throughout reentry former addicts are struggling with a somewhat more difficult and stressful experience.

Subgroups

The twenty-one former addicts fall into three relatively distinct subgroups in terms of when initial heroin use occurred. The *immediate users*, the nine boys who used within the first ten days after release, can be seen as succumbing to the initial and most immediate pressures towards heroin use. Two-thirds of all initial use (nine of fifteen users) occurs during this early reentry period, which corresponds roughly to the "transition period" described in Chapter 6. For the six *late users*, initial use did not come until quite a bit later, somewhere between three and four weeks after release. These boys managed to survive the immediate pressures, and their initial use resulted from a somewhat different set of factors.

---

[4] All differences reported are significant at the .05 level or better.

The final group of six boys, the *nonusers*, did not use heroin at all during the reentry period.

The following analysis examines the experiences of these groups in order to identify both the pressures towards relapse at different points in the reentry period and some of the factors that may have helped support abstinence. First, the most immediate pressures towards relapse are discussed, drawing primarily on the experiences of the immediate users. Next, the experiences of the late users are examined to identify factors precipitating heroin use later in the reentry period. The final portion of the chapter attempts to identify some of the factors that supported abstinence. The reports of the nonusers will first be examined for indications of why they were able to abstain completely. Then various aspects of the life situations of the immediate users will be contrasted with those of the late users and nonusers. Taken together, the late users and nonusers represent those who successfully survived the immediate pressures towards relapse and in this sense can all be considered relative abstainers. These comparisons reveal certain life situation factors that seem to facilitate abstinence.

Pressures toward Immediate Use

Some instances of immediate drug use appeared to represent a relief from the difficult uncertainty and tension of the question "Will I or won't I end up using again?" Anyone who has tried to quit smoking should understand this pressure, particularly if they have tried "cold turkey," or immediate and complete abstinence. Struggles with this tension seemed to be significant for about a third of the former addicts. This kind of tension demands to be resolved quickly, and the only quick resolution is through heroin use. This pressure stems in part from the belief held by most of these boys that heroin use was in fact an all-or-nothing thing, that they would either be "straight" or "strung out." But it was also heightened by the nature of the release situation, which abruptly confronted the boy with temptation while providing little prior opportunity to test out motivations and little concurrent support for abstinence.

The uncertainty of the question of use represents a relatively direct struggle with heroin as a problem in its own right. Yet it is much more appropriate to view drug use during reentry as a *response* to other problems rather than as an issue in and of itself. For every boy, heroin use was imbedded in the context of other reentry problems and was not an isolated event. Moreover, in important ways heroin use represented a familiar, readily available, and somewhat effective means of *coping* with other problems, which the boy either utilized or had to resist. For what kinds of specific problems, then, is heroin used as a coping response, and what does it offer as a solution?

One immediate problem was described in an almost straight stimulus-response framework. Seven boys (five of them immediate users) reported that as soon as they got out they reexperienced, in at least mild form, withdrawal symptoms. They felt nauseated, nervous, had chills, etc. They describe what sounds almost like a conditioned reaction to the old stimulus environment with which withdrawal had previously been associated. In fact, several of them reported it as directly related to returning to their old neighborhood, where they had gone through withdrawal before. Moreover, the seven actually identified here may underestimate the number experiencing this reaction, since the first report of this experience occurred too late to include it as a question in many interviews. The possibility of this being a more widespread experience is suggested by the significantly higher level of physical symptoms reported by former addicts. Taken together, these data indicate that one of the immediate pressures towards heroin use is the relief of physical symptoms that are in part conditioned responses to old environments associated with heroin withdrawal.

This suggests as well that previous environments will tend to elicit a variety of former responses associated with these environments, whether they be physical reactions or more in the realm of feelings, attitudes, expectations, and behavior patterns. This may help explain the rapid loss of motivation experienced by some boys immediately after release. It clearly indicates the folly of expecting that removing the boy from his environment and "cleaning him up" will have much effect on his heroin problem unless he is also helped to achieve new ways of responding.

For some boys heroin was used to deal with the general stresses of transition and reentry, to relieve anxiety, nervousness, fear, depression, etc. For example, one boy, who used on the second day, reported that he was overwhelmed by the frantic pace of life on the outside and felt very anxious and depressed. A friend offered him some dope and he "just did it." Another boy used heroin to "kill depression." Heroin is clearly relaxing and takes one away from the hassles and pressures of the world. In the short run it is relatively effective in dealing with many of the previously discussed stresses of transition, and it is a readily available alternative.

Some immediate users used heroin as a way of relating to friends and of fitting in. A pervasive reaction to reentry was a feeling of estrangement, of being out of it, and of feeling strange with former friends. Accepting and using heroin offered by a friend provided a very easy way for relating with him, both because of the familiar activity involved and because of the easy-going feelings created by the drug. Heroin use can provide the releasee with a smooth reentry into outside relationships and with a sense of belonging.

By the same token, abstinence can alienate boys from their friends. Many boys indicated that they felt "out of it" precisely because they weren't using drugs when their friends were. Before prison these relationships had centered around heroin use and were not really available afterwards if the boy would not participate in the heroin use. This was a serious problem when few alternative relationships were available, which was frequently the case, since preprison lives as junkies had pretty much restricted friends to other addicts.

Another problem to which heroin use is an attractive response is having nothing to do. Complaints of boredom were frequent during the immediate transition period and some immediate users indicated that boredom was one reason for their use. Heroin use offers a pleasant, relaxing, and familiar activity with which one can fill time. In similar situations, some of us might go to a bar and drink, watch TV, or read. The last option was generally not attractive to these boys, and for recreational purposes, getting high may have some real advantages over drinking and TV. In light of the "emptiness" of reentry discussed in Chapter 6, the use of heroin to meet recreational needs cannot be discounted as an important factor. Putting the argument differently, if they really had something better and more interesting to do, they might turn less to heroin.

The concern with nothing to do also reflects the ambiguity and lack of direction of initial reentry. For the same reason that many boys look to jobs to structure and give direction to their postrelease lives, many boys feel pressures to turn to heroin use. It can offer a set of activities, feelings, and relationships that structure lives in familiar ways.

The central argument of this section is that it is necessary to view initial heroin use during reentry as a readily available and somewhat effective way of coping with some of the immediate problems and pressures of reentry: physical and emotional stress, alienation, and boredom. It is tempting to treat heroin use only as an attempt to escape from problems. The problem with the "escapist" perspective is not so much that it is wrong as that it is seriously incomplete. It does not adequately recognize the seriousness and difficulty of reentry pressures, nor does it give full due to the short-term effectiveness of heroin use in coping with them. Heroin does relax; it does help one relate and fit in; and it does help to fill time and organize one's life. Most important, the "escapist" view acknowledges neither the immediate accessibility of heroin use as a response nor the serious absence of available and supported alternatives for coping with transition pressures.

Late Use

The group of late-users is particularly small because two of the six were not available for the final interview; their late use was reported by their mothers. The four cases, however, offer important contrasts with the other groups.

In all four cases, initial heroin use came right before the B3 interview. These boys seemed to have used heroin out of the frustration of mounting difficulties and lack of visible progress despite serious efforts to "make it." Their use came after long, frustrating periods of waiting for jobs to materialize and after sincere efforts to avoid contact with former addict friends. For three of them, abstaining had been a difficult struggle throughout. In two cases, there was increasing family conflict and tension as parents began to doubt the sincerity of the boys' job search and his claimed abstinence. In a third case, the boy's girlfriend's parents considered him nothing but a junkie and persistently interfered in his relationship with the girl.

However, job frustration seemed the key factor in triggering initial use. One boy used immediately after his fourth job rejection. Two others had just settled for lousy jobs, both under pressure from parole officers. One took a part-time job at a car wash and the other, who was twenty-three, enrolled in the local CAP agency work crew program for teenagers. There was no sign for any of them that satisfactory employment was developing, and they seemed to respond to this failure as a sign of their inability to make it. Their drug use seemed to represent the beginnings of giving up on attempts to change in light of the predominance of frustration and failure they were experiencing. It is perhaps the late users, more than either the successes or early failures, that indicate most clearly the need for immediate opportunities for change and clear signs of success.

Nonuse

In the generally pessimistic reentry situation described so far, the real question may be why any boys *are* successful in abstaining. It is a difficult question, because most of the six nonusers confronted stressful and frustrating situations similar to those who used. Two complained of real loneliness as a result of avoiding addict friends. Two complained of extreme frustration in finding jobs, and two others found working full time quite difficult. One was living in a family situation of high conflict and parental distrust. In fact, these boys did not represent clear successes. In only three cases did continued abstinence appear at all likely. The basic issue was the same as for late users: in light of continuing frustration and difficulty, would there be enough support and sense of progress to enable them to maintain efforts at change? Yet they had managed to abstain longer than the others; what had enabled them to do so?

Basically, the nonusers had more positive elements in their lives to provide the needed support and confirmation that change was possible. All but one described quite positive family situations, relatively free of conflict and involving substantial trust from parents. Two had quite close and supportive relationships with their families, and three others reported less affection but felt they were given free rein and were treated like adults. Only one was caught in the cycle of conflict and distrust so frequent in the postrelease family relationships of both addicts and nonaddicts.

Though two had been consistently frustrated in attempts to get jobs, the other four began working during the first week, had relatively well paying jobs, and had been doing well at work. They saw their jobs as an important concrete sign of their ability to make it. This superior work situation is the clearest concrete difference between the late users and nonusers.

Four of these six boys had a close relationship with a nonaddict friend, and all four said that these relationships were important aspects of their success. What may be most important is that in three cases these friends were working full time themselves and thus provided support not only for abstinence but for work efforts as well.

None of the above factors in and of themselves totally distinguish these boys from those who used. Yet, though it is impossible to work out any kind of "total score" to compare users and nonusers, more of these factors seemed to dovetail for the nonusers and provide the critical supports for their abstinence.

Immediate Users Compared with
Late and Nonusers

Both late and nonusers successfully resisted the immediate pressures towards use and in this sense are all relative abstainers. Indeed, it is not unreasonable to consider them as essentially similar groups, particularly given the tenuousness of the abstinence of at least half of the nonusers. Comparisons with the immediate users reveal some important differences in life situations, primarily in peer and family relationships, which may help explain both early relapse and initial abstinence. As explanations for the various patterns of heroin use, these differences are only suggestive, since they may reflect consequences as well as causes of differential heroin use. They do indicate important differences in reentry experiences between the groups.

The importance of the availability of nonaddict friends as support for abstinence is suggested by these comparisons. Seven of the twelve late users and nonusers described a close relationship with a nonaddict friend, whereas only one of the nine immediate users did. These relationships were with girlfriends, relatives close in age (cousin, brother-in-law), or with nonusing friends from preaddict days. These relationships were either present at release or began within the first week out. In all cases, they were reported as important in the boy's efforts to abstain. These friends gave the boys someone to do things with who did not draw them into contact with heroin, and they provided replacements for addict friends lost by abstaining. Without exception, these friends actively encouraged and supported the boys' efforts to abstain. In most cases, the boys saw these friends as important signs that they could break with the past. The virtual absence of such relationships among immediate users may be critical to their early use. Though the quick heroin use among immediate users may have precluded the development of similar relationships, it appears more likely that they were simply less available to immediate users. For example, girlfriends and relatives provided many such relationships for the late and nonusers. Among immediate users, however, three girlfriends and one sister were active addicts.

There also appear to be important differences in family situations. Three relatively distinct kinds of family relationships emerged during reentry: high conflict, laissez-faire, and close-supportive. (This analysis includes all thirty-four family relationships. See next chapter for details.) By far the worst were conflict relationships in which there was extensive conflict centering on issues of trust, supervision, and adulthood. Laissez-faire families at least treated the boy as an adult and let him manage his own affairs, while close relationships were openly positive and supportive. Immediate users were much more likely to be involved in conflict relationships with their families. Of the nine immediate users, seven had conflict relationships with their families, and none had close relationships. Among the twelve late users and nonusers, there were only four conflict relationships, whereas there were four close relationships.

To some extent, the family conflict of immediate users resulted from the boy's drug use. However, the patterns characteristic of each family type seemed to emerge quite early, usually before initial use. Families in the conflict group tended to monitor their sons' activities very closely, offer advice and warnings frequently, and be openly suspicious of any small signs of problems. This meant repeated ritualistic warnings whenever the boy was going out and a lot of questioning and checking up when he got back. These families, unlike the laissez-faire and close families, attempted to play a supervising and controlling role with their sons. It backfired, making the boy feel distrusted, treated like a child, and as though no one believed he could make it. The high incidence of such relationships among immediate users suggests that the parental behaviors involved may have contributed to difficulties with abstinence. In two cases, heroin was first used partly out of spite for unfounded parental accusations. In five other cases the boys own self-doubts were worsened by parental suspicions.

There are no apparent differences between immediate users and others with respect to employment, with about half of each group working by the end of the month (four out of nine immediate users, six out of twelve late users and nonusers). As indicated earlier, employment issues played a more direct role in late use than in immediate use. However, it is crucial to highlight that only one boy in the entire sample began using drugs *after* he started working (five began work after initial use). This suggests that having jobs immediately available at release may be critical to successful abstinence.

In summary, immediate use seems to occur primarily in response to the variety of transition stresses and problems of reentry. Heroin use is a particularly tempting response, because in many ways it provides at least short-term effective solutions to many of these difficulties. The findings just discussed suggest that the boy's ability to resist these immediate pressures depends considerably on the existence of supportive human relationships during the reentry period. Even a single supportive relationship from a friend or relative, a girlfriend, or the family appeared to make a considerable difference during this period.

The issues at the end of the reentry period are somewhat different. Initial heroin use at this stage followed serious efforts to make positive adjustments, especially in the employment world, and appeared to be a response to the mounting frustrations and failures encountered in these efforts. At this point, visible signs of progress, particularly securing a job, were perhaps more critical to continued abstinence than were supportive relationships. To sustain their efforts at change these boys needed concrete signs that those efforts would meet with reasonable success.

Conclusions

The picture of heroin relapse during reentry suggests the importance of viewing heroin addiction in the general context of a life style: the activities, attitudes, and relationships that integrate the individual with his social environment. Heroin addiction, particularly because of the way it is treated by society, defines and draws the addict into a very pervasive and far-reaching life style. It substantially structures his activities by demanding that he spend most of his time getting drugs and avoiding detection; it shapes his relationship to almost every person he knows; it restricts the range of people he has relationships with; it affects his health; it affects his family relationships; it defines his relationship to the legal structure; it determines his goals and relationship to the future; and it shapes his attitudes toward himself. In short, drug addiction tends to organize one's whole life within its own set of rewards and negative consequences and within a highly structured social role.

What are the implications of this perspective for understanding the issues of heroin use during reentry? As we have seen, the basic experiential task of reentry is that of "fitting in," of achieving some sense of social integration with the outside world. Heroin use provides a very effective solution to this problem. It can organize the releasee's whole life by defining activities, tasks, and goals, by structuring relationships to others in familiar ways, and by providing its own meaning, excitement, and direction. In the ambiguity and uncertainty of reentry, heroin use offers almost instant identity and structure. It may not be a totally comfortable solution and is certainly not free of major problems, but neither is any other solution. At least it provides a social role and identity that is familiar and consistent with what the addict has come to believe about himself and the world. In the short run, before its negative consequences have accumulated, it may well offer more excitement and meaning than the marginal conventional alternatives available to most releasees during reentry.

Yet it is important to recognize that the basic problems faced by released addicts are not primarily problems of addiction per se. As this chapter should have made clear, the problems that provoke postrelease drug use are basically the same problems that confront nonaddicts: the transition stresses immediately following release, and later in the reentry period, the need to settle the question of how to fit in, and the issue of whether real change in life style is either possible or worthwhile. These struggles arise in the context of the same concrete problems as for nonaddicts: alienation from friends, the availability and meaningfulness of jobs, conflicts with families about trust and supervision, the lack of concrete supports and payoffs for changed lives, etc. Though some are intensified by the drug factor (e.g., family conflicts), the addict is basically not struggling with a unique set of problems. The struggle with heroin use per se revolves primarily around the fact that heroin use is an available and effective solution to many reentry problems.

This suggests that the major focus of helping programs for the addicts during reentry should not be that different than those for nonaddicts. The situational stresses that both groups confront are essentially the same, and unless they can be effectively addressed, it is unlikely that the particular attitudinal and behavioral responses of the addict himself will be open to change. Most important, meaningful and supported alternatives need to be developed to compete with the effectiveness of heroin use in meeting the individual's community reintegration needs. It is difficult not to conclude that the major question facing the returning addict, particularly at the end of the reentry period, is, "Why *not* use?" for he is finding few alternatives that offer him as much as heroin use does.

10 Reentering Family Relationships

Mothers expect you to be a goddamn priest.
Ron Stanley

He's driving me crazy. I'm a nervous wreck, and I don't think I can stand it much longer.
Mrs. Stanley

It is important to recognize just how crucial the family is during reentry. First, the family is a critical immediate resource at reentry. Boys leave the institution with very little money, usually without jobs, and with very low skill levels. As an immediate source of room and board, the family is essential. Second, though many have already lived on their own, most will need whatever stabilizing influence an adult family residence can provide during the first several months of release. Although probation and parole are in the background for about two-thirds of these boys, they are generally ineffective and the family is really the only stabilizing influence available. Finally, along with girlfriends in some instances, the family is the only potential source of caring and belief in the boy during his struggles with adjustment. Indeed, one of the major pressures on family relationships is that the family is really the *only* available resource for meeting *all* these needs.

Characteristics of Families

For this study, a family was considered to be any family residence with an adult present assuming some responsibility for the boy. At release, all but three of the boys were returning to live with families that had raised them as children, including one foster family. The other three boys were going to live with close relatives with whom they had lived at some time in the past. Twenty-three of the boys had been living with these families immediately prior to incarceration. The other eleven were returning to live with their families after living elsewhere six months or more prior to incarceration.

By the end of the first month, seven boys were no longer living with the intended family of residence. Three had left because of serious family conflict. The others had left to live with other relatives, and all maintained close contact with their families.[1] Two others had been returned to jail.

[1] In all cases, the policy was to conduct the second interview with mother of the intended residence. No attempt was made to interview anyone from the new residence.

These families were probably typical of a reformatory population. In only seventeen families was an adult male present, though in all families there was an adult female present. In eight of the families there was one stepparent present. Though these variables were not a focus of this investigation, correlations were run contrasting on all measures families with and without "fathers" present and with and without stepparents present. There were no indications of important differences. Finally, though no specific measurements were taken, it was very clear that all but a handful of the families were poor, with probably a half struggling with serious poverty.

Dynamics of Prerelease Relationships

The purpose of this section is understanding the prerelease dynamics of family relationships and the kind of initial family reentry situation they create. Certain aspects of preprison and prison relationships are discussed as they bear on this major question. The overall picture can be sketched very quickly. As viewed from the point of release, many of the conflicts and tensions of the past seem to have passed, and the prison relationship has either raised, or threatened to raise, hopes that things will be different and better after release. Yet both parties face the reunion with a great deal of uncertainty, and because of real differences in the nature of self-interests and self-protective needs, boys and mothers tend to respond to this uncertainty in different ways as they anticipate the future. The boys tend to respond to their hopes and the mothers to their doubts. Each response is fundamentally realistic.

View of Past Relationships

There is a good deal of variability in the kinds of preprison relationships described, ranging from intense conflict to relatively positive relationships. In part this variability is due to many of the boys not living at home immediately prior to incarceration. The most typical description by those boys who were at home was of substantial tension and conflict. Both boys and mothers attributed most of this difficulty to the boy's delinquent activities.

The boys almost uniformly refused to blame their families for their own delinquency. Only seven say the family situation had anything to do with their getting into trouble, and only two say that they are angry with their parents for what happened. At this point the boys accept major responsibility for their own plight, saying they caused far more trouble for their family than it caused for them.

The mothers say that they felt ineffective in influencing or controlling their sons, either because their sons overtly rejected their attempts ("He wouldn't listen; he just got angry") or because he just did what he wanted ("He listened, but then did what he pleased"). Most reported that such patterns had existed for years, and the typical comment was, "There was nothing I could do—it was out of my hands."

By far the worst situations were described by mothers of the addicts, since these boys' difficulties can reach into the home more. Many said that their sons' simply did not seem like themselves anymore, neither physically nor emotionally, and that it was virtually impossible to communicate with them. They reported incessant day and night phone calls and visits from friends. Some discovered their sons shooting heroin with friends in the home. Many said their sons had stolen from them, and this was confirmed by the boys.

Prison Relationships

As was shown earlier, visiting by families was frequently very difficult. The institution itself was inaccessible (forty-five minutes to two hours from most homes), and many families had difficulties arranging transportation. Visiting hours were very restrictive. At the beginning of the study, visits were limited to two two-hour visits per month on weekdays only (evenings, weekends, and holidays excluded) but were changed halfway through the study to allow up to four one-hour visits per month with visiting hours extended till 7:00 P.M. Only half the families were able to make the maximum number of visits allowed, and eight boys received a total of two or less visits.

Incarceration had two different effects on family relationships. For a substantial minority, about 25 percent, the effect might be described as "out of sight, out of mind."[2] These families had made little attempt to visit or write and seemed to have forgotten about the boys. These families were the ones most caught by surprise by their son's release. In most cases, the isolation fostered by imprisonment fed into a characteristic relationship between son and family in which the family had given up much sense of responsibility for the son, though they had not necessarily given up caring about him. There is no question that the institutional exclusion supported and exacerbated this response of "out of sight, out of mind."

Imprisonment had a different effect when the family maintained some reasonable level of contact; prison contacts raised hopes. A variety of circumstances surrounding visits in prison both create a sense of improved current relationship and raise, or threaten to raise, hopes that things will change for the better in the future. Both boys and mothers reported improved relationships during imprisonment. Two-thirds of the boys and half of the mothers said the

---

[2] Glaser (1964) uses this phrase to describe the effects of incarceration on peer relationships. The effects on family relationships he describes as "absence makes the heart grow fonder." The present findings indicate a more complicated picture of family relationships.

relationship was better, whereas only one boy and one mother said it had gotten worse.

At the same time, the circumstances of prison do not give secure grounds for fully believing in these hopes. There are clear external pressures for positive interactions. A number of mothers said, "Visiting is not a time to argue about anything. You both are trying to make the other person feel better." Given all the unhappiness surrounding imprisonment, there are pressures on both parties to put their best faces forward in order to make the visits as positive as possible. In fact, less than a fourth of either the boys or the mothers reported any arguments or upsetting experiences at all during visits. The situation tempts one to believe that everything is better and things will be different in the future.[3]

Expectations Concerning the
Postrelease Relationship

Mothers' Attitudes at Reentry

The best indication of the mother's feelings were their answers to the question: "Have you been worried about your son while he has been at the reformatory?" A typical response was, "No, I have been *less* worried. It has been a time of peace of mind." Fully 50 percent of the mothers reported feeling less worried while their sons were in prison. Hence, their sons' imprisonment meant a real *respite* from the worries, problems, and responsibilities of having him at home. Other comments make this clear:

"I haven't had to panic every time the phone rings, thinking it was the police."

"I haven't had to worry about him getting hurt or killed when he is out running around with his 'friends' at night."

"There haven't been a bunch of junkies calling here at all hours of the night."

Their son's return meant the resumption of these worries and responsibilities. When asked directly if they were worried, 75 percent admitted that they were. There was a real and understandable reluctance to go through the same hassles and to resume the same responsibilities all over again. Part of each mother resented having her life seriously disrupted again. But it is not easy to give up parental roles, and this compounded the ambivalence. Most mothers were

[3] Mothers of drug addicts are affected the most. They respond to the changes in their sons' manner and appearance. He has regained weight, looks neat and healthy, can be talked with, and looks and acts like himself again. But other than these superficial appearances, the mother has no basis for judging whether he has really changed or not and is caught in the cruel dilemma of either hoping against her best judgment or of being cynical about her own son's future.

genuinely glad that their sons were getting out of jail, and many looked forward to seeing him around again. They also felt a good deal of guilt. Their reluctance to resume responsibilities was difficult to deal with when they knew that if they didn't assume the responsibility, no one would. The question of whether things would be different this time became critical. Yet they found themselves without an answer. When asked how things would go after their son's return, most said, "I don't know what to expect. I'll just have to wait and see." Two-thirds refused any more definite prediction than this.

They had little basis for being more definite. The prison situation forces one to base judgments only on superficial appearances and on verbalized intentions that threaten to raise the mothers' hopes. But they had learned from hard experience to distrust such signs. Again, typical responses to questions concerning their son's motivations about staying out of trouble were, "I don't know. His intentions are *always* good but he never follows through. I just have to wait and see." Or "I can just hope. He *talks* like he's changed, but then he always *sounds* good." The prerelease situation permits no more evidence to either boy or mother than good intentions and leaves both confronting a good deal of uncertainty.

The Boys' Attitudes at Reentry

The boys' want to—have to—hope for the best. They are extremely dependent upon the family at release and are simply not in a position to admit to any doubts or question about their families. Hence, prior to release, they are genuinely repentant and refuse to blame their families for problems of the past. They tend to hang onto the hopes that prison relationships have fostered and voice relatively positive expectations concerning the future. When asked how well they thought things would go with their families, they all said either "good" or "okay." None said they expected much conflict.

Yet though they indicated little doubt, neither did they evidence much enthusiasm. Generally the boys, just as the mothers, hoped for changed relationships, but at some level seriously doubted that it would happen. The difference between the boys and their mothers is that the boys hoped more and hid their doubts better.

Both boys and mothers face family reentry with raised hopes and serious underlying doubts. Data from the intercorrelational analysis strongly suggests that the boys resolve this uncertainty in the direction of their hopes, while the mothers resolve theirs in the direction of their doubts (Appendix). Mother's estimates of the future relationship are highly and consistently correlated with their ratings of the past relationship and not at all with their ratings of the prison relationship. This suggests that they expect the future to be not really different from the past. For the boys, however, exactly the opposite is true. Their estimates of the future are correlated with their evaluations of the prison relationship and not at all with their judgments of the past. This suggests that boys' expectations are based on their prison relationships, which they described as changed and improved. Moreover, the boys themselves seem aware that their mothers' expectations are based more on the nature of past relationships than on prison relationships. They were asked to rate how they thought their mothers' would react to their return. *These* ratings correlated with their own evaluations of past, not prison, relationships.

This pattern reflects differences in the self-interests and necessary self-protective measures of boys and mothers. If the boys want to make it after release, they must hope that things will be different this time, and this includes hoping that relationships with their families will be better. Mothers, on the other hand, have been badly burned in the past by believing promises that "this time things will be different." Particularly when they feel impotent to affect what happens, they need to protect themselves against further hurt by anticipating the worst and assuming that things will eventually turn out the way they always have.

The circumstances surrounding family reentry have created a potentially negative self-fulfilling prophecy. The boy's family holds essentially negative expectations, and the boy already seems aware of these expectations. Though both boy and mother are willing to try to make things different, in most cases, it will take very little to confirm these underlying doubts.

A potential source of conflict is indicated in the responses of both boys and mother to the question of how the family might help during reentry. The mothers were essentially unsure. The only specific answer they could come up with, other than providing a place to stay, was to offer advice and guidance to the boy. Boys responses either focused on mothers simply being understanding and supportive, or were put in terms of their mothers *not* doing something, in particular not counseling or supervising. When boys were asked how their families might make reentry more difficult, over half said by being on their back or always giving advice. Thus, what is clearly negative for the boys is the one thing that mothers feel they can offer: advice and counseling. Moreover, the mothers are not thinking in terms of the kind of help the boys mention most frequently: simple support and understanding.

Initial Family Relationships

The initial week at home was quite positive. Boys reported being pleasantly surprised at how well things were going. With few exceptions, both boys and families seemed to be trying hard to make things go well and to suppress any doubts and suspicions they might feel. The boys' B2 reports on family relationships are the most positive of any of the interviews.

The boys' descriptions of positive and negative aspects of initial relationships follow the pattern set at B1. Half speak of positive aspects in terms of less nagging, supervising, and arguing than previously, while the other half point to new positive qualities: more trust and understanding and better communication. There are some complaints as well. About a third feel that their parents are "bugging them" or "on their backs" a little too much: about looking for a job, staying out too much, and associating with the wrong people. The boys' reaction is that they know what they have to do, will do it if they are going to do it, and don't want their mothers bothering them. They don't want needless advice, particularly when their parents don't really understand what they are going through.

For seven or eight boys the family is very difficult to cope with. In four cases, there is open and serious conflict around issues of heroin use, either because the boy used and was found out, or because the mother was unjustly suspicious and accusing. These relationships were all rapidly deteriorating. In three other instances, there was a serious question of whether the boys' parents cared much about them at all. But these serious problems are not typical. On the whole the first week is a good one, with about 80 percent of the relationships positive and satisfactory.

Postrelease Family Dynamics

By the end of the first month family relationships are not nearly as positive, and more than half are openly and rapidly deteriorating. One can now classify about 60 percent of the relationships as essentially problematic and only 40 percent as relatively positive. This represents a substantial shift from the 80 percent estimated as positive at B2. The significance of the deterioration is seen in the fact that by B3 three boys have left home because of family conflict and up to five others are seriously considering doing so. Five others are also talking of moving out on their own for a variety of reasons, including less than satisfactory relationships at home.

The Boys' Perspective

From the boys' point of view the critical issues with families are trust, emotional support, and adulthood. What the boys both want and need most during reentry is for their families to care about and believe in them, to trust them, and to treat them like adults. How families relate to these needs is crucial to determining the boy's family experience and its impact on him.

By B3, it is possible to characterize families in terms of different styles of relating to these persistent themes. Boys who rate their family situations as "good" do so in one of two ways: they either say that the family lets them alone and they can do what they want, *or* they say that they feel closer to their families and describe a supportive relationship. Those who rate their family relationships as "poor" describe a good deal of open conflict, complain of too much advice, or, more seriously, indicate anger about constant checking up on them. These three types of family situations might be labeled "laissez-faire" relationship, "close" relationship, and "conflict" relationship, with seven families in the laissez-faire group, eight in the close group, and seventeen in the conflict group (two boys were unavailable for last interview).

Laissez-faire Relationship

The boys themselves characterize these relationships in terms of the absence of parental efforts at supervision, control, and advising. The boys feel left alone and free to do what they want. Parents put no pressure on them in terms of curfews, friends and activities, though they may insist the boys work and contribute to the family. At the same time, the boy indicates no particular closeness or warmth in the relationship itself. The issue of trust never arises one way or the other, and the boy usually feels treated like an adult. In about half these cases, this freedom seems to disguise a lack of parental investment in the boy, and the boy may feel the parents don't care. In the other half, however, contacts with the mother indicate that she cares but is not particularly close with the boy and sees him as having the major responsibility for his own life. The central characteristic of this group is that the boy is left very much on his own in terms of whether he makes it or not.

Close Relationship

These are the most positive and promising family relationships. The boys usually say that they feel closer with their parents than before and that they feel that there is better understanding and better communication. The boy receives' encouragement to do the right things but in ways that make him feel trusted and treated like an adult. He also has a good deal of freedom, but parents seem in touch with what is happening in his life. The central characteristic is that it is a close, supportive relationship.

Conflict Relationship

These relationships involve extensive conflict. The boys complain of parents "being on their backs," of unneeded advice, of unwanted supervision and control efforts, of parents whose every effort to influence the boy makes him feel untrusted and treated like a child. The boys feel their parents are rapidly becoming accusing and suspicious. The severity of the conflict ranges from those who find the family an additional irritant in an already difficult reentry experience to those who are só angry they are ready to leave home as soon as possible. This group ranges from well-meaning parents whose every effort backfires, to situations where the conflict reflects very deep issues of caring and responsibility. The central characteristic is high conflict and distrust.

The conflict families represent the norm or baseline during reentry. Not only are conflict relationships the most frequent (over 50 percent), their difficulties reflect the kinds of problems reentry imposes on all families, whether they manage them well or poorly.

Some of the conflicts are an almost inevitable result of living with parents, as is highlighted by the relationships of those who were *not* living with parents. Five of the boys in the close group were not living with their mothers but with other relatives (an uncle, an older married sister, etc.) while remaining in close contact with their mothers. Interestingly, these boys' relationships with both their mothers and their residential family were the best of any and, by contrast, provide some insight into the sources of problems in other families. These boys reported very positive relationships with their mothers. They reported talking with their mothers more than did other boys and said they were willing to listen to advice. They said their mothers talked *with* them rather than "counseling" or checking up on them. They seemed free to enjoy the relationship itself. These mother-boy relationships seemed to be free of the mutual demands of a mother-*child* relationship. The mother did not feel compelled to exercise parental control and was freer to maintain interest and concern in him. The boys did not feel that everything they did would have a direct impact on the mother. In short, their mothers were able to provide primarily an supportive relationship, someone who cared for, believed in, and encouraged them.

In their residential family, these boys were less prone to interpret advice or household regulations as implying distrust or childishness. Boys and these relatives were able to relate as adults, and advice was received as a sign of interest rather than suspicion. Moreover, these relatives seemed less ready to examine the boy's behavior for signs of slipping back into old habits. In short, these relationships were much freer from the influences of the past: traditions of distrust and the conflicts of parent-child relationships.

These family situations were different from others in two important respects. First, issues of supervision and of "responsible" behavior were severed from the mother-child relationship, with the result that boy and mother were free to form an important close relationship, while the relatives were able to provide steadying relationship on relatively adult terms. Second, the more intimate residential relationship was relatively free of a history that doomed it to repeating old patterns of conflict and distrust.

Conflict families present a very different picture. Mothers felt it necessary to provide parental supervision, were quick to examine behavior for signs of slipping back into old habits, and tended to take any of the boy's mistakes personally. Boys were prone to experience the resulting advice as infantalizing supervision and to interpret even minimal supervision as a sign of distrust. The parent-child relationship and its history of conflict quickly set up a vicious circle of self-fulfilling prophecies and prevented a satisfactory supportive relationship.

Probably the worst part to the boys were the parents' attempts to supervise them. Not only did they find this infantalizing, they also experienced it as ritualistic and irrelevant, as one case well illustrates. This boy (twenty-one years old, actually) returned to live with his elderly grandparents, who had raised him as a child. Though he had been living on his own for some years, they still seemed to feel it their duty to discharge parental responsibilities now that he was back. They, as he put it, "counseled" him constantly, telling him what to do and what not to do, telling him not to use drugs, not to associate with bad people, to get a job and stay out of trouble, to stay off the streets, etc. They were ritualistically doing their "duties" as his residential parents. The boy was having a great deal of difficulty adjusting, and this constant harassment was very hard on him. His grandparents knew very little about of what he was going through, in his mind or on the streets, and their supervision seriously worsened his problems. A number of boys reported feeling that their mothers gave advice and checked up on them because it was their "duty" as parents, which they experienced as ritualistic and as not involving any real understanding of their difficulties.

Another pressure reported by several boys was that their mothers cared *too* much about what happened. A frequent comment was, "Sometimes I wish she wouldn't care so *much*." Many boys felt that the smallest variation in their behavior had a strong impact on their mothers and that they could hurt their mothers a great deal. The intensity of a mother's concern could exert a lot of pressure on the boy, during a period when things would not always go well, and inhibit the freedom he needed to make, and learn from, mistakes.

It is helpful to examine these issues in terms of how the family situation meshes with the boys' needs. The boys clearly need both adult supervision and a supportive relationship. Yet it may be impossible for most families to fill both roles. It is quite clear that parents are not, and cannot be, effective supervisors. These boys are too old to accept parental supervision, and parents' efforts to do so simply precipitate old patterns of conflict and resentment. Such efforts prevent mothers from playing the role they might most effectively play, being someone who supports and believes in the boy without maintaining vigilance over his misdeeds. This is what the boys repeatedly say they need and want from their families, and the small group living apart from their mothers illustrates how meaningful such a relationship can potentially be.

Yet it appears difficult for most mothers to give up the role of supervisor, despite the fact that many resent having to resume this responsibility. In part they know there is no one else to assume this role if they don't, and in part they must feel that giving up this responsibility would reflect negatively on their commitment and concern as parents. The laissez-faire families are interesting to examine in this light. These mothers have adopted a realistic attitude, admitting that things are beyond their control and asserting that the boy is old enough now to make his own bed and sleep in it. This stance has some real advantages for the boys. They do not have hovering parents; they are given responsibility for their own behavior; and there is little conflict driving them away from home. Their mothers have pretty much given them free rein, other than insisting on reasonable responsibilities to the family. Yet the fact that the boys indicate little closeness or active support in these relationships suggests that the mothers may be unable to give up responsibility without also giving up concern, thus depriving the boy of a needed caring and supportive relationship.

Boys also need a residence that facilitates their sense of adulthood if they are to feel that satisfactory change in their lives is possible. In part they need to be free of old adolescent conflicts with parents. As important, however, is the need for a residence which recognizes and accepts that the major arenas of his growth occur outside of the family—in jobs, with girlfriends, and with peers. An adult residence is necessary for stability, at least in the short run, but it must be able to tolerate and support sometimes risky interactions with the outside world. The personal stakes for most mothers were simply too high for them to be able to grant this freedom.

From the Mother's Perspective

Most important to understanding the mothers' experience is the extent to which they are either willing or able to invest themselves in the problems of their sons. Over half say directly that they have either already reached or are about to reach the limits of their capacity to invest much of themselves—time, energy, resources, or caring—in dealing with the problems of the boy. They identify an issue that confronts most families, whether openly acknowledged or not. It can take several forms:

"He's got to work and contribute to the family if he wants to live here—I just can't afford to have him sponging off me."

"There's nothing I can do any more—if he's going to get in trouble, he's going to get in trouble and I just can no longer worry about it."

"He's driving me crazy; I'm a nervous wreck, and I don't think I can stand it much longer."

"If he gets in trouble again, I will refuse to bond him out or visit him in jail. It just reinforces his behavior and irresponsibility."

Their reasons for feeling this way are selfish but realistic. Most feel their sons are old enough now to take responsibility for their own behavior. They feel that they have been struggling with these problems long enough and that they can't, and shouldn't have to, deal with them any more. They often feel that they simply don't have the needed resources. They have their own lives and often other younger children to take care of. Some feel that they simply don't have the emotional resources to go through another set of crises.

In a few cases, the mothers are ready to turn their boy in if they suspect something, particularly mothers of addicts, and a few parents are ready to kick the boy out at the first sign of trouble. Such serious threats to the boy's residence are infrequent but present. Many will let him stay without much hassle until his problems begin to invade the home, but will not invest much of themselves in helping him. Many are still trying to discharge their parental responsibilities of guidance, supervision, and helping their boy out of trouble, but resent having to do so.

Very few of these mothers are capable of anything like an open-ended commitment to the boy at this point. Even in those cases where things are going well, mothers say their fingers are crossed because they are not sure how they would cope if things started to go badly. Most mothers simply have to be able to relate to these boys as responsible and independent adults. Yet they are deeply ambivalent, for it is not very easy for most mothers to abandon their parental responsibilities.

The dominant question in the mother's mind is, "*Has* he changed?" Near the limits of her tolerance and resources, she must answer this question quickly so that she can avoid being hurt and prevent the fruitless use of minimal material and emotional resources. Their question, therefore, is not "Will he be able to change?", which is more realistic since the boy is going through a *process* of change.

This situation pressures mothers to make rapid judgments. The boy's behavior is examined for signs of slipping back into old habits, and already at one month, many mothers seem to have already made their judgments. To the question "What changes have you noticed in your son since he's been out?" 50 percent say, "He hasn't changed a bit. He's the same as always" (meant negatively). In light of the confusing problems and experiences of reentry, this is clearly an oversimplification and rapid judgment. To be sure not all judgments were negative. Yet the mothers' self-protective doubts tend to make the boy "guilty until proven innocent," and negative signs speak louder than positive ones, for they are more consistent with underlying expectations.

Mothers also tend to interpret any misbehavior in personal terms, to see it as a sign that the boy really doesn't care about the family. To the question "Does your son seem to care more about the family now than before?" 15 respond, "He really doesn't seem to care at all." This tendency to personalize is certainly understandable. In the context of the difficulties reentry creates for them—

resuming responsibilities despite reluctance, having hopes raised despite doubts—it is easy to understand a feeling that a son wouldn't act like he does if he really cared about the family.

Under these circumstances, it is very difficult for the mother to meet the boys' needs. In a situation where he is bound to fail as frequently as succeed, in which judgments are made quickly and more readily on the basis of failures than success, and where his own doubts are very high, the boy has very little room for error. All too frequently the family situation interferes with rather than facilitates his change.

Conclusions

Despite the serious problems inherent in family relationships, it would be a mistake to conclude that the family cannot be an important and even positive resource during reentry. Not only do the boys need family resources, most families themselves, despite considerable ambivalence, are willing to try to be of help for a while at least. Two issues are critical to making this possible. First, it is necessary to see the family residence as indeed a transitional arrangement. These boys are at an age when they should be establishing substantial independence from their families, and both the boys and their mothers believe this. Neither feel that it is fair for them to have to once again be struggling with these long-standing problems. Hence, for most boys, the goal of moving out on their own in the reasonable future is both appropriate and necessary. Family problems would seem much more manageable to both the boy and his family if active steps were being taken toward the boy's moving out on his own.

Second, many of the problems in these relationships are exacerbated, if not caused, by the situational pressures of reentry and hence can be reduced by appropriate interventions. The single most important intervention would be providing help in securing and maintaining employment for the boy. Working is a critical sign of motivation and progress to both the boy and his family and provides both symbolic and financial independence. Also, prerelease help directed at getting both boy and family to recognize, define, and accept the nature and limits of their mutual responsibilities would go a long way to alleviating many problems, especially if it were made explicit that this was to be a short-term and transitional residential arrangement. Finally, providing an adult helping relationship would reduce the demand on mothers to provide supervision and control and would free her to provide the emotional supportive relationship needed by the boy.

11 "In Their Own Words"

This chapter presents the interviews done with one boy, Carl, and his mother Mrs. T.[1] They show how the various issues of reentry are experienced by the respondents themselves. The selection of the particular case was extremely difficult. Both boys and their mothers varied in their life situations, the problems they confronted, and in their articulateness and openness. It is almost impossible to choose a case representative of all of the important issues of reentry. Carl and his mother were selected both because of their articulateness, especially Carl, and because their interviews illustrate a wider range of issues than most. They are perhaps least illustrative of the intensity with which many others experienced the problems of reentry. For Carl, things went relatively well. In fact, he represents one of the most successful boys. He had a job immediately available at release and a family with sufficient resources for his return not to be a major financial crisis. They lived in a suburban area much more pleasant and promising than the oppressive urban ghettos to which most boys returned. The family relationship, though reflecting many typical problems, was not as bad as many. This case does not illustrate the serious crises of former addicts.

Nevertheless, Carl's and his mother's reports are valuable, because they bring out a variety of the important issues of reentry, albeit in a mild form. It is interesting to speculate on how differently things might have gone if Carl had not had a job awaiting him at release.

Carl was eighteen, white, and a solidly built six-footer. He was in the reformatory for seven months for a series of offenses, mostly drunk and disorderly conduct and breach of the peace, which had put him on probation before and eventually led to his incarceration. He returned to live with his mother, a teenage sister, and two young brothers. He had an older brother in the Marines who had served in Vietnam. His father was an alcoholic who had left home four years earlier and at this time resided in a nearby town. Carl rarely saw him. His mother worked to support her family and had taken a second part-time job in anticipation of Carl's return, which she would keep only until he started earning enough to pay for the added expenses of his return. They lived in a modest home located in a relatively attractive residential neighborhood of a middle-to-lower class suburb.

---

[1] The responses reported here represent the exact words of Carl and his mother. However, at several points the responses to a number of very specific questions have been combined into one statement. This was done to provide a more coherent and integrated statement of the general issues being explored than would be permitted by the disjointed series of responses to narrow questions. Throughout we have remained as true as possible to the sense of what the respondent was communicating and the specific words are their own.

Interviews with Carl

Interview B1

This interview was conducted one week before Carl's release. It was done in the reformatory library, with no other people present.

Interviewer: What do you think is going to happen when you get out and what will be the main problems you face?
Carl: The main thing is to go back to my old job. The problem will be getting back into the working habit, and whether I like that kind of job—making phone pipe insulation. I'm so used to having everything planned here, I'm not sure how its going to go. I want to go into the Marines in three months. Another thing is, I'm going back to my hometown, and I'm afraid the cops will hassle me. It happened to a friend of mine just two days after he got out. I have to try a different style of living, no everyday parties and that kind of shit. I'll have to make a big adjustment.
Interviewer: You'll be getting out next week, the twenty-third, right?
Carl: No, I'm getting out tomorrow, the sixteenth.

Next we discussed his release date, which he thought was the following day. My information said it would be a week later. When we checked after the interview, my information was right. He had not been informed that he had lost a week's good time for an infraction (stealing doughnuts from the kitchen to give to friends at Christmas) for which he had already spent a week in solitary confinement. He had had no idea there was any change in his release date.

Interviewer: How do you feel about leaving?
Carl: It'll be good to get out of here, but I'm a little worried—about whether I can make it and about not coming back here. I'm really glad to go, but this worry makes me hesitate. I thought getting short would be hard like it is for most guys, but it has been pretty easy. I thought it would never get here, but it has. It was just a little out of reach and now I can suddenly grab it. I've been thinking a lot about getting out of here the last few weeks, especially at night in my house [cell]. I've also been thinking a lot about my plans. This is important, because you need something to fall back on when you get out there. The more you think, the more you realize you've been here and need to remember it when you get out. No one here has talked to me about my plans. I've just talked to my mother on visits.
Interviewer: What are your plans for working when you get out?
Carl: My old job is waiting. I have a good relationship with my boss and he promised my job would still be there. My mother checked this out a few weeks ago and its okay. I've worked before. I was working at this job when I

got busted. Working doesn't really appeal to me that much. I only do it for the money, which isn't that great—$2.50 an hour. I'm really full of indecision now. If I found something I liked, I would like working. I'm always glad when I get back to work after being off, because it gets boring when you're not working. But the job is a real drag. I will just work a few months until I can get into the Marines. After that I might go to business college. I have a high-school diploma in a business course.

Interviewer: What do you want to do right after you get out?

Carl: I would like to relax and take it easy, like taking a burden off my shoulders. I want to do a lot of things I haven't been able to do. I want to spend as much time as possible with my family. If it seems boring, then I'll gradually go see people. I'm most worried about falling back into my old habits. I used to drink a lot and that worries me a lot.

Interviewer: How will things go with your friends?

Carl: I think pretty good. I've always been close with friends, and things haven't changed that much. We'll be glad to see each other. There are a bunch of guys I'm looking forward to seeing, and about five or six I really want to avoid. I think the main thing that will be changed on the streets is the drugs. I hear there is a big upward surge on it. I don't think my friends will get me into trouble if I avoid the ones I should. The hardest thing to avoid will be the large parties and dances. At parties punks come to make a name by fighting you and then you get a breach of peace. I used to go to those things high on pills or drunk and get into a lot of trouble. I know what to avoid, its just a question of will power.

Interviewer: Do you have problems with drugs or alcohol?

Carl: I have a slight drinking problem—I drink a lot. I didn't miss it here, but it worries me a little. The problem is that there is nothing to do in town but get drunk or high.

I've used drugs some—barbs, grass, speed once, and heroin twice, just chipping—back when I was in high school a year ago. I was never hooked, and I won't touch anything when I get out, except maybe grass. It won't be a problem.

Interviewer: How will things go with your family?

Carl: I'll be living with my family for just a few months until I get in the Marines. Here I discovered just how much I neglected my family and how much I miss them. We used to fight all the time. My mother was always on my back and I was bucking her. Then when I turned sixteen, it kind of let up; she let up, and I did pretty much what I wanted. I really only came home to sleep at night. My mother rode me some still, but I just wouldn't listen to her. I used to get really mad when there was fighting in my family, and I would leave. But my family had nothing to do with my trouble—I brought that on myself. When I started getting in trouble, my mother got angry but always tried to help, she was always ready to back me up. She used to blame herself a lot. Toward the end, though, she really started to get disgusted.

My mother and sister have visited me here a lot. The separation has really helped both sides—it has brought us much closer and I know it will help me when I get out, just the relationship itself. My mother is glad I'm getting out, but she's probably worried about whether I've learned my lesson. I think things will go okay with my family. There will only be hassles if I start back in on my old habits. I think she thinks I'm going to make it.

Interviewer: What are you going to have to do in order to go straight?

Carl: I really want to make it this time and I think I will. I definitely do not want to come back to this place. The main thing will be to keep away from old habits and a few select people.

Interview B2

This interview was done on a Sunday afternoon, in the living room of Carl's home, nine days after he was released on his delayed release date.

Interviewer: So what has it been like to get out?

Carl: Pretty good. The first couple of days my brother was here on leave from the Marines, and I spent most of the time with him. Saw a bunch of my friends. I was real disappointed in the changes in them—most of them are into dope. They used to be really tight, and now there are splits and factions and fighting because of dope hassles. I hate it. No problems with my drinking. I've had some but didn't get drunk like before. No problem with being moderate, like I was worried about.

Interviewer: So what happened about your release date?

Carl: I checked with my counselor, and he had it down for the sixteenth, like I thought, but in his file was a note saying it had been changed to the twenty-third. Mr. C. was supposed to tell me. When I asked him why he didn't, he just said, "Tough." You were supposed to know." I said I was doing hard time and could I call my mother to see if she could visit that night. He told me to write a letter. I was about to really blow my cool when I saw the superintendent and told him the story. He let me make a call and said he would try to get me out a few days later. When he didn't, I knew he said it to cool me off. It worked—time went okay till I got out. I just hoped there wouldn't be another fuck-up.

Interviewer: What was it like leaving?

Carl: I got out about 10:30 Friday morning and rode home with my mother and brother, who was home on leave from the service. It felt really good walking out the gate, like being born all over again. It was kind of strange riding home, being in a car again, with just my family and no screws around. We just talked about anything that came up—joked about my extra time. I was supposed to go right to see my parole officer, but I was wearing my prison shoes—my mother forgot my regular ones—so I decided to go home first and call my officer. He wasn't in and I left a message.

Interviewer: What was it like coming home?

Carl: It felt real good, but a little strange too. The house seemed a lot smaller. I played with my little brother—he showed me his toys. I took a shower, went out to see a buddy and his wife. Came back for lunch and then out to do some shopping. Back for dinner, and then back to my buddy's till about 1:00 A.M. We listened to records, drank, talked. It was enjoyable, not exciting.

Interviewer: Tell me the main things you did each day during the week you've been home.

His report indicated mostly riding around with his brother, seeing friends, relatives, some shopping. He went out with a girl a couple of times and spent a couple of evenings with a friend who was an addict. Gary didn't use any dope with him, but his friend was busted a few hours after he left one evening, which scared the hell out of him. The two most significant incidents during the week seemed to be a party he went to and his going to work.

Carl: I went to a party the night after I got home. Saw all my buddies. It was really depressing, seeing how everybody changed. I walked out with about five enemies. Well, not really. I just said the truth about certain people, and they weren't used to it, didn't like it. Like how stupid one guy was to be shooting dope. I was also needling people in the old ways, and they are not going for it anymore. Like I kidded one guy about when he was going to get engaged, and he told me he had broken up with the girl. I got into an argument with a girl who was cheating on my friend in the joint. About three or four people really jumped on me about it. I was really depressed after the party, seeing how they had all changed. Nobody was friends anymore. Everybody only cared about himself. The next day I just hung around the house.

I went back to work on Thursday [sixth day out]. That was a real drag, I didn't like it at all. I just didn't remember how much I hated that job, cutting foam insulation. There's no challenge—you're just programmed for it. I wanted to wait longer before starting, but I started feeling funny about staying out this long. I was supposed to start Monday, but I wanted to spend some time with my brother and relax a little. My boss said I could start any time, but I started worrying about my parole officer, and I was getting worried because I was starting to just hang around and it was getting dull.

Interviewer: What kinds of things have been hard to get used to?

Carl: The changes in everybody. They seem really hard to get in with. And so many are using dope. Also, I'm really impatient more than before. If someone is late, I get really impatient, like I'm afraid they won't come. Getting back to work is another hard thing, especially into that kind of work. And then deciding whether to stay there or not. I have to make a decision about working or going into the Marines, and I have to make it quick, because I really have to grab onto something quick. But I can't make up my mind.

Interviewer: Say some more about your friends.

Carl: Well, like I said, its been kind of tough. They were glad to see me, but not as much as I thought, and I think its really because of the dope. They're hustling and friendship doesn't mean much. Most of them aren't really strung out, like most are working. They don't really have bad habits. They just don't seem to care about anything. I just don't want to spend as much time with them as I thought I would—don't want to fall back with those guys. I've gone out a couple of times with this girl I knew from before. She's just good company. I double with a friend. He's into dope, but we get along.

Interviewer: How are things going with your family?

Carl: Pretty good. I thought it would be a little better than it is. A few more hassles than I expected. Mostly about my friends. She already thinks I'm getting back into the same old habits with the same old people. She knows a lot of them use dope, like the kid I double with. She seems to think their bad habits will rub off onto me or something. She doesn't realize that things aren't as bad now as when I was in jail. They boiled over and aren't so bad now. She thinks I'm staying out too much and says I'm no different than before. We've actually only argued a couple of times. I kind of expected a little of this. I do think my family will be an important part in whether I make it. My mother could help most by just being natural and easy.

Interviewer: What things should other guys be prepared for about getting out?

Carl: Working! Getting back to a job is tough. Also people, getting back with people. There is a different atmosphere, and its hard getting used to a lot of new people as well as your old buddies who have changed.

Interview B3

Interview took place four weeks after Carl's release.

Interviewer: So how is it going? What to your mind are the main problems you've faced since getting out?

Carl: It's going pretty good—about the same as last time. I'm working everyday. Working is still my main problem. There's a lot of other things I'd like to do. It's the same job, and I'm just keeping myself there. Still not sure how long I want to stay.

Interviewer: What's the problem with your job?

Carl: I don't mind working that much, but I don't like the job. But I'm getting used to it. Days used to drag, but now I'm falling into it. I don't like hanging, and this keeps me in money and off the street. It's basically for the money right now, which is getting tight. I charged $80 worth of clothes and $60 at the dentist, plus social expenses. It's hard. And they screwed me on the pay. Before jail, I had gotten a raise to $2.50, but they wouldn't let me keep it.

I'm getting $2.25. But I plan to stick with it a few weeks to see if I can get a raise. I'll quit if I don't. I missed three days the week before last. Just called in sick and took off. I just wanted to do other things—just rode around with some buddies. Then I regretted it because I didn't have any money and I've gone every day since. My mother was screaming and raising hell. She had her say and that was it.

Interviewer: What's happening on the street these days?

Carl: Not much really. I mostly just go out with my chick, double with a friend. Sometimes I go to a bar where some buddies are. I just don't see much of my friends. No more problems like when we talked before. No hassles, and I don't feel out of it anymore. I'm still dating the same girl. I see her several times a week. During the week I go to her house, and on the weekend we double. It's good fun, but nothing serious. But it's really good being with girls after so long. It has really brightened things up. It's a real hassle having my license suspended though, because I always have to look for a double.

Interviewer: Any problem with alcohol or drugs?

Carl: No. I'm not having any trouble with my drinking. I just drink occasionally and haven't gotten drunk. I haven't smoked any grass since the first time. I was going to do some acid a few weeks ago but decided not to. I could take or leave drugs, but would rather leave them.

Interviewer: How are things going with your parole officer?

Carl: He seems like an all right guy. I've only seen him once. He said he wouldn't break my balls. He was Mr. Nice Guy. Of course, I haven't been in any trouble, so I don't really know. He said he'd help me get in the service and didn't mind if I changed jobs. He hasn't done anything to help me, but he seems okay.

Interviewer: How have things been going with your family?

Carl: Worse than before, but its okay. We've been having more arguments. She bitches about something and blames me, like about using too much hot water, and I tell her what I think. It's stupid. Just like old times. I've threatened to leave a few times and she says go ahead. That used to happen all the time before. But it passes quickly, and we're laughing an hour later. She gives me too much advice, but I know she's worried about me. I don't get my back up unless she's telling me what to do about something she knows nothing about. Seems like she was expecting an angel to come home. She wants me to stay around the house all the time. Of course, I'm not really doing what I planned, I mean staying around the house more. She doesn't want me to leave my job, and I tell her that that is my business. I didn't really expect these problems, but overall she hasn't made it more difficult for me. I think this is the best place for me to stay.

Interviewer: So how does it feel to be out now?

Carl: It's good. Haven't thought much about it recently. The novelty of being out is over now. Working is a real drag, and sometimes it's hard to find something to do if I'm not with my girl. But it's no big hassle. I don't think being in the joint hurt me at all. Actually it helped me. It made me realize what a fool I had been, that the life I was living was pretty stupid.

Interviewer: Do you feel like you've been making any progress since you've been out?

Carl: Some. I don't feel like I'm doing much with this job. I'm just kind of staying out of trouble. My mother wants me to get in the army right away. She doesn't want me just hanging. She sees it as the answer to everything. But I want to stay out a while longer. At least one more month.

Interviewer: Now that you have gone through it, what do you think other guys should be prepared to face when they get out?

Carl: Well, I'd say number one is be prepared for getting back into hassles with your parents. Number two is to get yourself to stick with a job and not say fuck it. Having a steady chick really helps. It takes up time and its fun.

Interviews with Carl's Mother, Mrs. T.

Interview M1

This interview was done in Mrs. T's home, three days before Carl's delayed release date.

Interviewer: First, I'd like to find out how much information you've gotten about your son's release arrangements.

Mrs. T.: I thought he was supposed to get out last Friday, the sixteenth, but he called me the day before to say he would get out the next week. He told me he lost some good time for stealing those doughnuts at Christmas. I called his parole officer and asked him to find out why they changed the date. He said the same thing Carl did, so I guess it's right. It upset me. It seems to me that a week in that hole is punishment enough.

No one except Carl ever told me anything about his release date before this happened, but I didn't doubt it until this. His parole officer called me to tell me he would be Carl's officer, but he didn't say anything about what would be involved.

Interviewer: I'd like to ask about the kind of communication you have had with the reformatory staff while Carl has been there.

Mrs. T.: I haven't had many questions to ask, really. I wanted to talk to the superintendent about the possibility of Carl getting into the Marines, but it was too difficult to get time. I asked his parole officer to check out the confusion on Carl's release date, and he did. I also asked him about Carl getting into the Marines, and he said it wouldn't be possible. No one from the reformatory ever contacted me about anything, and I never talked with any guards when I visited. One thing did happen that upset me. Carl was in the hospital with hepatitis, and I didn't find out until I visited. They should have told me.

Interviewer: Have you had a chance to talk with Carl about his plans?

Mrs. T.: Yes. He wants to go into the Marines like his brother and then go to college after the service. I'd like to see him do what he wants, as long as he works. I'd like to see him go to college. I think his plans are okay, but it doesn't seem like he can get into the Marines. I talked with his former boss, and he said he could have his job back when he got out.

Interviewer: Has it been difficult to visit with your son?

Mrs. T.: It's a strain with me working and with the younger children. They won't let the little children in the visiting room, and they wouldn't let me and my oldest daughter split up our visiting time so one of us could stay with the children. One time the guard complained when I brought Carl *two* toothbrushes and a *blue* washcloth. I have been able to visit twice a month regularly. I never missed a time, but I don't think Carl realized how difficult it was.

Interviewer: How did the visits go that you had?

Mrs. T.: He used to cheer me up. Except that visit on Christmas Eve when Carl came out of the hole for the visit. He seemed really cold, and it worried me a lot that he would have to go back when I left, especially since it must be really cold in there. We never had any arguments or anything like that on any visits.

Interviewer: Have you been worried about what was happening to him at the reformatory?

Mrs. T.: Not really. In some ways I worry less about him in there, since I don't have to wonder about where he is, and what he's doing. I was a little worried that he might not behave in there. Sometimes he is foolish and comical.

Interviewer: What do you think caused him to get into trouble before?

Mrs. T.: He went along with the crowd. He just didn't have the strength of character to say no. I took him to a psychiatrist once who said he had a weak character like his father. His father is an alcoholic.

Interviewer: Did you know about it when he was starting to get into trouble? Did you feel like you could do anything about it?

Mrs. T.: I didn't know at first, but I had an apprehensive feeling. I didn't have any control over him then. He was out all the time, every night. Half the time he didn't even come home for supper. I tried talking to him, I tried hitting him, I took him to a psychiatrist. But he wouldn't accept any help.

Interviewer: Do you ever feel that he's angry at you because he's at the reformatory?

Mrs. T.: No. He knows that it was something that he brought on himself. I did all I could to help him.

Interviewer: Before he went there, how did you feel things were between him and the family?

Mrs. T.: They were very strained. He didn't act like a member of the family. He didn't contribute at all, and he was never here. We had a lot of arguments, but we cared about each other. We argued the most about his never being here and about his drinking. He drank a lot and hung around with the wrong crowd. And his appearance was terrible. It's been a lot calmer and more peaceful since he's been away.

Interviewer: Did you feel like he understood the kinds of problems you were having?

Mrs. T.: I don't think he cared about my problems. No, I guess I think he cared a great deal, but didn't realize it and didn't show it.

Interviewer: How do you think your relationship has been with him while he's been at the reformatory?

Mrs. T.: It's a lot better. He shows more respect and understands his responsibility to his family. He understands better what I tried to tell him. He realizes how important his family is.

Interviewer: How do you think things will go when he comes back? How do you feel about his coming back to live with you?

Mrs. T.: I think things will be pretty good. He seems a lot more cooperative now. I'm not worried about what will happen. I want him to come back here, until he can get into the Marines. I know he's looking forward to coming home. We may have some arguments, especially if he starts hanging around with the wrong crowd. I'm not worried about his drinking though.

Interviewer: What are your biggest concerns about his coming home now?

Mrs. T.: I'm just worried that he might get back into the same crowd again, but I really think he's less likely to get into trouble now. I think his attitude has changed. The biggest thing is whether he is mature enough.

Interviewer: What will you do if if you think he's starting to get into trouble again?

Mrs. T.: I would want to get help for him before he's put away. I would go to his parole officer if it wouldn't get him into trouble. I think he might listen to me now. I just hope he cares enough about me to stay out of trouble.

Interview M2.

This interview was done in Mrs. T's home four and a half weeks later. Carl had been out one month.

Interviewer: How do you feel Carl is doing so far?

Mrs. T.: I think he could do better. He hasn't been getting into any trouble, but he could work more. I thought he would work faithfully and help me pay the bills, but he's a poor manager of money. He's not doing as well as I expected, but I don't like the word "worse." But at least he's working. That's more than most of them do.

Interviewer: What are his plans at this point? What would you like to see him do?

Mrs. T.: I think he will eventually go into the service in a couple of months. He continually talks about getting a better paying job, but this is foolish if he is going into the service soon. I think the service would be excellent for him. He's doing nothing now but stagnating. He's doing nothing beneficial. He doesn't like his job, and I don't blame him. Really, I'd like to see him do whatever he would like.

Interviewer: What kinds of problems do you think he is having? What is he going through?

Mrs. T.: I'd say he's having a ball. I wish he would slow down. He's always on the run—he just eats, sleeps, and goes. He's out every night till midnight. I don't know what he does. He doesn't tell me. I take it for granted he's with his girl. He should spend more time with his family. His younger brothers would like to see him more.

Interviewer: Have you noticed any changes in him since he's been out?

Mrs. T.: When he got out, he expressed more care for the family, but he hasn't stayed here at all. He soon forgot how much he cares for the family. I'd say he's irresponsible. He's always trying to borrow money from me, but he'll have to learn to budget.

Interviewer: How has he been getting along with you since he got out?

Mrs. T.: I'd say pretty good, but he never gives me the time I want with him. He won't listen to my problems. We've had some arguments, but he's not around enough to have very many. We had one big one, but I forget about what. I told him I thought he had changed, and he told me he thought I had changed. I told him to move out and he said he would. But it passed. I also told him he forgot awfully quickly how much I visited him at the reformatory.

Interviewer: How much do you feel you've been able to help him since he got out?

Mrs. T.: He wouldn't be able to manage if he weren't living here. And I take him to work and try to talk to him about money. But he doesn't listen much better than he did before. He doesn't give a damn about my advice, never has. I try to treat him as an adult, but he's not mature for his age.

Interviewer: Do you feel like you can trust him?

Mrs. T.: I do trust him. Not with my charge account, but as far as behavior goes, I trust him.

Interviewer: What are your biggest concerns at this point?

Mrs. T.: I wish he would understand that my concerns are for his benefit. I would like to see him do something with his life, like go into the service and into college. I'm pretty sure that he is not getting into trouble again. I think he's going to do okay, I just know he's not happy with his job.

12 Conclusions and Recommendations

This final chapter discusses the kinds of changes in correctional practice needed to ensure more effective community reintegration of released offenders. We must be quite clear about the major issue which these recommendations must address. The fundamental problem of reentry is not so much the offender's needs and problems during this period as it is the negligence of those correctional agencies responsible for meeting these needs. Unless both researchers and practitioners recognize this negligence as the central question of reentry, there is little hope that change efforts will go beyond the development of a few experimental programs and result in changes in general correctional practice.[1] This stance is particularly important given the role that community reentry programs are playing and will continue to play in the community corrections movement. If they are to help shape the new directions in corrections, they must come to terms not only with the offender's reentry needs but also with the reluctance of corrections to assume responsibility for reintegration.

The correctional agencies bear far greater responsibility for the failure-guaranteeing situation confronting offenders at release than do the individual offenders. The institutional and situational factors surrounding release create a situation with which anyone would have difficulty coping, let alone those with minimal personal resources. It is a situation that almost systematically interferes with the inmate's ability to anticipate and prepare for the problems of reentry. It creates a very abrupt and confusing immediate transition period. It distorts both positive and negative anticipations in ways that increase the difficulty of coping with postrelease realities. It heightens the perceived stakes of short-term failures in ways that lead to quick discouragement. It provides no help in developing new alternatives for more productive community adjustments. In short, the management of reentry enforces an abrupt confrontation with a bewildering array of problems while providing the individual with none of the supports and resources necessary for dealing with them. Indeed, the individual psychological and behavioral patterns make most sense as relatively realistic adaptations to powerful situational realities.

---

[1] The discussion in this chapter makes the assumption that the correctional neglect of reentry revealed in this research is not atypical of general correctional practice. There is little reason to assume that it is, the existence of certain visible exceptions notwithstanding. The previous studies of reentry summarized in Chapter 1 all indicate the lack of effective attention to reentry problems. In addition, several people with wide exposure to corrections in this country, including both researchers and correctional administrators, have read this manuscript and indicate that this is a typical picture.

Most important, it is a situation which is largely immutable through individual action. The individual offender has no influence over those correctional practices that contribute to his difficulties and has little ability to create opportunities when they do not already exist. Though the individual may have the power to adjust his attitudes and behavior to social realities, he has little individual power to adjust those social realities to conform to his needs. If the situation he confronts is one in which the social realities do not come close to meeting his legitimate needs and aspirations, then the major responsibility for meeting those needs rests squarely on those institutions that have the resources and leverage necessary to this task. It is for this reason that the reluctance of correctional institutions to assume this responsibility is the major issue of reentry. And it is because the "reintegration" model recognizes this responsibility, when it asserts that crime is as much a reflection of social failure as personal failure (see Chapter 1), that a discussion of correctional neglect of reentry cannot be divorced from the more general issue of corrections' commitment to the reintegration model.

Commitment to Reintegration: Myth or Reality?

The critical question is why this correctional neglect of reentry exists. It is a particularly important question to consider in formulating action recommendations in the context of research such as that presented here. There is little question that the recommendations that follow most directly from the research findings themselves would concern the kinds of helping strategies and programs needed in light of the problems of reentry identified by this research. Indeed, it is not difficult to generate a list of changes needed in correctional practice or to generate a reentry program "blueprint" based on the current understanding of reentry problems.

The problem comes when one begins to question whether new program ideas are what is needed to produce more effective correctional approaches to reentry and reintegration. Such recommendations would both make and reinforce the assumption that the basic system's problem, the reason underlying correctional neglect, is ignorance—of the needs and problems of reentry, and of effective helping strategies. At a more general level, such recommendations would both reflect and reinforce the assumption that the underlying problem is primarily a technical one, involving a need for more sophisticated problem analysis, better program design and evaluation, better organizational communication and efficiency, etc.—problems that can be solved by a more sophisticated application of social science technology.

Though it may appear to be stating the obvious, there is serious question as to whether the problems either of "alternative" program development or of general correctional change are fundamentally technical. Burdman (1969), himself a correctional administrator, states that the real issue is not a need for "new knowledge through research" but the nagging question: "Why are agencies not applying what is already known?" He provides several examples of well-documented findings that have not found their way into correctional practice. For example, despite substantial evidence that moderate differences in length of sentence have no impact on subsequent offense behavior, most courts and parole boards show little inclination to reduce unnecessarily long sentences. Or, despite substantial evidence that at least 30 percent of state prison populations could be safely managed under minimum custody, most states maintain virtually all inmates under unnecessarily restrictive security conditions. His examples are convincing. There are far more "good ideas," supported by solid research, than are ever put into practice. Yet the fact that Burdman immediately states that what is "needed now is a more detailed model for future planning of community-based correctional systems," and then proceeds to supply one, suggests that the "nagging question" is not being adequately addressed and that technological solutions are still seen as the answer.

Burdman's article is not atypical. In the document "The Future of Corrections" (Conrad 1969), a major statement of the community corrections movement, most contributors pay homage to the substantial resistance that will be met in instituting innovation and change, and frequently even relate that resistance to entrenched vested interests in current practices and to society's moral and political attitudes (essentially political issues). Yet the recommendations presented by these contributors, both researchers and practitioners, are overwhelmingly technological: professionalization of personnel, the need for criminal typologies and differential treatment approaches, designs and reports of model programs, calls for systems analyses, long-range planning, and careful evaluation research. With but one or two exceptions, there is little attempt to address the more political issues of why existing knowledge does not get put into practice and to formulate action recommendations with these issues in mind. Without for a moment denying the importance of the technological issues mentioned, they reflect the implicit assumption that the problems of innovation and change are fundamentally technological ones, not political ones. This assumption is also seen in the substantial recruitment by federal agencies (e.g., LEAA, NIMH) of social scientists into correctional change work, with their heavy focus on research, experimental program development, and program evaluation.

The critical question that seems to remain largely unaddressed is whether the problems of change are not more political issues of societal priorities in the distribution of resources and commitment to different classes of people. That is, to what the extent are the correctional system and other critical social institutions genuinely committed to really serving the interests of the offender, when that commitment means, as the reintegration model implies, the redistribution of resources from the "haves" and the "have-nots"?

It is a question not only of whose interests are being served by existing structures and procedures but also of whether the offender's interests will be any better served by reform movements. The past gives us little comfort regarding the future. For example, if we reflect on the results of the previous "revolutions" in corrections discussed by Schragg (1971), we see that the change from revenge to imprisonment replaced chopping off a man's hand with chopping off major portions of his life. And from data collected in 1965, right in the middle of the Age of Rehabilitation, we find that most institutions have very few personnel professionally trained for this work: 17 percent of workers in juvenile institutions, 6 percent in adult institutions, and 3 percent in jails and facilities for misdemeanants (Corrections Task Force Report 1967). One must raise seriously the question as to whether the Age of Reintegration will serve offender's interests any more effectively than have these previous "revolutions."

Platt (1969) raises more systematically the question of whose interests are served by reform movements by turning to an analysis of the "child-saving movement" of the late nineteenth century. This crusade played a significant role in the formation of the juvenile court, the training school, and the reformatory— all of which are currently under severe criticism for creating as many problems of delinquency as they solve (e.g., Forer 1970). The crucial part of Platt's analysis concerns the motives underlying that movement. He argues that it reflected less a break with the past than an "affirmation of faith in traditional institutions" and served primarily to further both "symbolic and status functions for native, middle-class Americans." It is a convincing illustration that there is little reason to assume that reform movements are fundamentally intended to serve the interests of the offender, and Platt himself goes on to raise serious questions as to the motives and political interests being served by current correctional change movements.

With respect to the community corrections movement, the fundamental question is really not whether institutions will eventually be replaced by community-based facilities. Indeed, we are in substantial agreement with Goldenberg (1972) that despite setbacks and substantial political resistance, this transition is likely to be accomplished on a relatively wide scale. The fact that this movement in corrections is paralleled by similar deinstitutionalization movements in the treatment of both the mentally ill and the mentally retarded suggests that it reflects a more general social trend in the nature of deviance control in our society. The fundamental question in the community corrections movement is whether these changes in form will be accompanied by the changes in ideology and practice necessary to effectively serve the interests of the offender himself. Specifically, the issue is whether the motives and self-interests of those involved in this movement will even permit a serious commitment to *reintegration* in its most basic sense, i.e., a shift from an exclusive focus on offender change (treatment and rehabilitation) to an equal emphasis on institutional change.

Even a brief look at the two social institutions that are now, and will continue to be, most directly involved in shaping the community corrections movement—the correctional system itself and the mental health professions—raises serious doubt as to their commitment and capacity to seriously address the fundamental institutional change tasks of the reintegration model. Ryan (1971), for example, marshals convincing evidence that the criminal justice system is far less engaged in administering equitable justice than in protecting the status quo. He observes, as have others, that far more time is spent maintaining social order than enforcing laws. Through a look at the nature of existing laws, their selective enforcement, and the powers that tend to control the criminal justice system, he concludes that a major social function of this system is the protection of the political and economic interests of those in power. Yet it is in large part these very forces that control the resources necessary for effectively meeting the reintegration needs of offenders. If one takes his analysis seriously, it is hard to see how the correctional system itself can be effectively committed to changing those very forces that control it and whose interests it functions to protect.

It is convincing in this regard to observe that much more impetus for prison reform comes from prisoners themselves than from the correctional system. It is only when their active rebellion makes the political costs of negligence too high for elected public officials that any attention or resources are directed at the long-standing and serious problems in our prison system. And unfortunately, political interests are usually better served by repressive measures than by reform efforts.

The involvement of the mental health professions in community corrections provides little cause for greater optimism. As Goldenberg (1972) argues, the community corrections movement will attract a major involvement on the part of the mental health and mental-health-related professions, both because substantial money will be available and because the community corrections movement is quite consistent with the increasing importance of a "community" orientation within these fields themselves. Though the involvement of these professions will help to insure the long overdue and quite welcome shift in corrections from a punitive to a more humane rehabilitative approach, there is serious question as to whether they possess either the conceptual or practical tools for the task of reintegration. As has been amply discussed before (Szasz 1960; Ryan 1971), these professions tend to bring a fundamentally "medical" perspective to bear on human problems, which focuses primarily on the individual and intrapsychic determinants of those problems and interprets them as problems of *psycho* rather than *social* pathology. Hence, the involvement of these professions is likely to insure that any alternative settings that replace institutions will be primarily clinical in nature and directed primarily if not exclusively on treating or changing the individual offender, both because of the conceptual orientation of these professions and because they possess the skills for only this task. The major risk, therefore, is that these professions are likely to provide the community corrections movement with a basically "victim-blaming" rationale and technology, which will help divert attention and effort away from the more fundamental institutional and social change tasks of the reintegration model.

The intent of this discussion has not been to present a thorough analysis of these issues but simply to argue that there is serious question as to whether the motives, self-interests, and orientations of those most involved in the community corrections movement reflect any genuine commitment to the institutional and social change tasks that represent the core of the reintegration model. Indeed, in one's more paranoid moments, it is not difficult to infer a de facto if not intentional collusion between the correctional system and the mental health professions to avoid this fundamentally political task. There is at least much to suggest that the negligence of correctional agencies concerning the reentry needs of released offenders stems less from an ignorance of problems and effective helping strategies than from the lack of a genuine commitment to address the fundamental issues of reintegration. Though there are perhaps no definitive answers to these questions, it should be clear that the stance one takes on them will influence considerably one's view of the intervention strategies necessary for ensuring effective attention to the reintegration needs of released offenders.

The immediate task of this chapter is to make suggestions as to the necessary characteristics of effective reentry programs. However, its purpose is not simply to propose the kinds of programs necessary for addressing the immediate reentry needs and problems of offenders but to suggest the characteristics of settings that we might view as truly alternative models of correctional practice, settings that will play some role in attempting to ensure that the community corrections movement confronts the fundamental tasks of reintegration. Hence the recommendations made will reflect not only the helping strategies implied by the problems of reentry identified in the present research but will also reflect a particular stance on the questions raised in the preceding pages.

These recommendations will be made in two parts. First, we will suggest the characteristics of programs necessary for effectively meeting the immediate needs and problems of reentry. We will then separately propose those characteristics that would be necessary to viewing those programs as truly alternative models of correctional practice committed to reintegration.

Characteristics of Effective
Reentry Programs

The following recommendations focus on general principles that need to be followed in developing effective reentry programs, particularly if they are to relate to the problems and process of reentry as experienced by the released offender himself.

1. Programs must begin with the assumption that most releasees are genuinely intent on changing their lives. Dembo (1971) argues that releasees are placed by the agencies that deal with them in the position of having to prove their interest in rehabilitation; they are considered guilty until they prove themselves innocent, and this contributes to rapid discouragement. The present findings strongly suggest that most offenders are genuinely concerned with "going straight" and that they initially perceive reentry as an opportunity for change in their lives. Motivation was more influenced by their belief in the possibility of change—meaning belief in the availability of alternatives, belief in their capacity to achieve them, and belief that their efforts would be supported by others—than by lack of concern with going straight. Programs must begin by assuming a genuine concern with change if they are to avoid self-fulfilling prophecies of failure.

2. The immediate reentry period, the first three to five weeks after release, appears critical to the nature of postrelease adjustments, and programs must focus their most intensive help during this period. There is little leeway for delay in providing support, since feelings and events move quite rapidly. This period is decisive to motivation, and critical events occur that threaten important initial resources, particularly jobs and family residence. Programs must try to ensure that meaningful opportunities are available immediately upon release to provide structure, direction and, most important, a sense that meaningful change is possible. Maximum individual help in managing personal and life-situation difficulties is necessary during this time.

3. However, it will be even more fundamental to eventual success for programs to begin working with clients several weeks to several months in advance of release. Reentry, both as a psychological and institutional process, begins prior to release, and much of the groundwork necessary for postrelease success must be done before release.

The boys repeatedly mentioned the importance of having some plans or objectives in mind to guide them during reentry. Programs should begin well before release to help the inmate assess problems, formulate plans and realistic objectives, and specify concrete strategies for achieving them. The inmate should become engaged in taking steps to implement his plans, such as contacting employers or job-training programs, talking straight with families, and upgrading educational skills. Such work can be done more effectively prior to the actual crisis of reentry, and any progress made will reduce the crisis nature of reentry.

Individual helping relationships should be well established prior to release. Their influence during the reentry crisis will depend considerably on the familiarity and trust established ahead of time. It is an important time for staff to demonstrate their commitment to the client and their capacity to follow through on that commitment. Staff should also get to know their clients and their life situations thoroughly before the reentry crisis period.

The length and intensity of prerelease work will depend somewhat on the type of reentry program. It should be particularly critical to nonresidential programs (e.g., advocacy programs) in which the postrelease influence will depend primarily on the individual helping relationship.

4. Programs must recognize that the primary source of reentry difficulties is the releasee's life situation rather his own personal limitations, attitudes, or emotional difficulties. The present research has identified an almost overwhelming array of such situational problems. This is not to deny personal difficulties of adjustment but to emphasize that the major sources of those difficulties lie more in the situational characteristics of reentry than in the psychological "hang-ups" of the individual. Reentry programs must know that life situation directly and in concrete detail, must focus interventions directly on those situational problems, and must direct their work with clients primarily towards facilitating their capacity to deal with them.

5. The major focus of these efforts must be on providing meaningful opportunities. The greatest need is for supported alternatives to previous life styles rather than supervision or adjustment-oriented counseling. We are referring to meaningful jobs or skill-training programs, educational opportunities, living arrangements that facilitate independence, and positive social and recreational opportunities. Moreover, these opportunities must not be second-class ones. If they are to be experienced as superior to previous life styles and worth struggling for, they must offer more than second-class community status and the possibility of staying out of jail. Making such opportunities available in ways that match the releasees interests, needs, and aspirations and then facilitating his skills in making use of them is the most significant task facing reentry programs.

5. Another major need is for an individual adult helping relationship that provides continuity and active support throughout reentry. The releasee needs someone whom he feels is committed to his own interests and believes in him. This person should be much more an "advocate" than a counselor, providing active help in managing problems rather than adjustment-oriented counseling. He would monitor release proceedings, help plan for release, help develop jobs or training programs, provide liaison with family, employer, and other community people, and provide guidance and support after release. Though helping the releasee to assess his own attitudes and personal problems, he would also provide active help in manipulating those agencies and institutions that control the releasee's life. The releasee needs someone actively "in his corner." The traditional counseling relationship with its passive, listening role and its primary focus on psychological problems is inadequate.

6. Programs need to recognize the extent to which change in one life sphere influences the others. Most important, though jobs and education are the cornerstones of successful reintegration, programs cannot neglect other needs interrelated with these. Releasees tend to confront the sacrifices of change before evolving a supporting life style that makes these sacrifices worthwhile. The releasee needs a social life that supports full-time work. However, efforts at

change are probably made worthwhile primarily by the quality and support of relationships with family members, wives, and girlfriends. Programs must be prepared to help the releasee manage these relationships.

7. Help with family relationships is especially critical. The present research indicates that for the youthful offender, families are both the single most important resource available during reentry and a major source of conflict and stress. Hence they can exercise either a major positive or negative influence. To facilitate family relationships, help should be provided directly to the family itself, for they have real reentry problems of their own. At a minimum, programs should help prepare families for their son's release. Programs should also facilitate better prerelease communication between releasee and family and better anticipation of potential problems. Most important, the major responsibility of guidance and supervision should be taken off the family's shoulders, freeing them to provide emotional support. Program staff should in most cases form relationships directly with the family so that they can be supportive to the family itself. Given the releasee's concern with independence and adulthood, and the family's own limited resources, the family should be seen as a transition resource while the releasee is preparing for independent residence. When available, residence with nonparental relatives can provide a very supportive reentry living situation.

8. Developing postrelease vocational and educational placements that are experienced as leading to meaningful future opportunities may be critical to a program's ability to engage the youthful offender.[2] Both because they are younger and have spent less time in prison, they may resist more than older offenders accepting the marginal status in society that is the typical fate of released offenders. They may be less willing to accept "stop-gap" or "shit work" jobs, as opposed to placement in educational or job training programs. They may also be more able than older offenders to sacrifice some short-term income in the interests of the future potential of training programs. Though truly meaningful opportunities should be the objective of work with releasees any age, this may be more critical to engaging the younger offender who refuses to believe that he can't get more out of life than those limited conventional alternatives typically available to him.

9. Finally, reentry programs should significantly involve agencies and people from the releasee's community. It is they who will confront the consequences of

---

[2] The author is currently conducting a survey of all community-based reentry programs for adult offenders in Massachusetts, of which there are about twelve. With only one or two exceptions, all of these programs report that it is the youthful offender that is most difficult to work with. They find him frequently uncooperative and resistant. They say, mostly with some reluctance, that these young men seem to need to spend more time in prison in order to realize the necessity of doing something about their behavior. The assumption seems to be that these are irresponsible and antisocial youths who have not yet realized the negative consequences of their behavior. An alternative interpretation is that they refuse to accept the legitimacy of a correctional process that they see as attempting to force them to accept a marginal status in society.

the offender's return and who will have to provide many of the resources, opportunities, and supports necessary for satisfactory reentry.

Characteristics of Genuine Alternative Reintegration Programs

This final section suggests six characteristics necessary for a setting to be a genuine alternative approach to the task of reintegration. These characteristics assume that the major issues of reintegration are more political than technological. Hence it is a setting's stance, in action as well as rhetoric, on the ideological and political issues raised earlier which is central to its representing a genuine alternative approach. These criteria are meant to apply not only to community *reentry* programs but to any correctional program that claims to be addressing the task of reintegration.

1. First, the setting will itself make the explicit assumption that the central tasks of reintegration are fundamentally political, whether that refers to the institutional and social change tasks of the reintegration model or to the issue of ensuring that corrections itself assumes a genuine commitment to this model. This means that the first task of that setting is to articulate its own set of social and political assumptions about the nature of the problems and the process of change with which it is involved. This ideology will provide the framework within which the setting will assess issues and determine its actions, both with respect to the setting's external context (the correctional system, the community, etc.) and with respect to its internal context, (its own motives, objectives, actions, staff-client relationships, governance, etc.). Hence, the setting will both guide and evaluate itself within an explicit political context.

2. Its intervention objectives will place as much emphasis on institutional change as on the individual remediation of its clients. Hence, it will recognize in its actions as well as in its rhetoric that the problems of reintegration must be confronted not only in the offender himself but also in those social institutions within which he leads his life. This means that the setting will not limit its institutional interventions to the needs of individual clients but will seek to influence the general policies and practices of critical social institutions: employers, educational institutions, service agencies, and the criminal justice system.

3. A truly alternative setting will take seriously the responsibilities of its role in influencing the nature of the community corrections movement and will recognize that its own contributions must extend beyond simply providing a new program model. It will therefore become actively involved in efforts to influence the correctional system, the nature of other "alternative" programs being established, legislative action on correctional issues, etc. In these efforts it will participate in alliances between other groups, programs, and individuals that

share similar points of view regarding correctional change. These will include other alternative programs, inmate and ex-offender organizations, relevant community groups and agencies, and individuals wherever they may be found. In general, this stance will reflect a recognition that genuine correctional change demands the collective political action of those who share similar self-interests and points of view.

4. It will develop an alliance, rather than a treatment relationship, between staff and clients. Staff and clients will participate with shared power and responsibility in shaping the setting's ideology, in the governance of the setting, and in its actions on both individual and institutional change. Such an alliance is necessary if the setting is to be honest to its view that the problems of reentry reside as much in social institutions as within the offender himself. More important, it recognizes that neither the setting itself nor any change efforts its participates in will genuinely serve the offender's interests unless he himself is fully involved in that process.

5. The setting will "not only be in but also of the community . . . It will lend and commit itself and its resources to community efforts to achieve self-determination" (Goldenberg 1972). The setting will therefore recognize that the needs, problems, and aspirations of its "clients" are not somehow unique and separate from the needs and aspirations of the community from which they come, and that ultimately, none of these needs and aspirations can fully be met unless that community and all of its members achieve the capacity for self-determination. Hence, the setting and all of its members, both staff and clients, will become actively involved with other community groups and individuals in attempts to address both correctional issues and other community needs.

6. Finally, the setting will be particularly alert to the dangers of social science, and especially mental health, involvement in the community corrections movement. While not dismissing their potential resources, the setting will nevertheless be ready to confront the tendencies of the social sciences to promote the view that problems of change are predominantly technical, to provide victim-blaming rationales for the status quo, and to reinforce elitist orientations (i.e., expert, "top-down" approaches) to institutional and social change.

It is clear that such a setting will almost inevitably be in conflict with its own sources of funds and with many of the agencies, particularly correctional agencies, upon which it in part depends for its effectiveness. It should first be noted that if this is true, then it is a clear indication of exactly that lack of commitment to the reintegration model that we have argued is the major problem to be faced in its implementation, and hence constitutes a strong argument for settings quite like the one that has been characterized here. The reality is, however, that the very nature of its functioning will place such a setting's existence in jeopardy. This has two implications. First, it means that such a setting will not pursue the goal of its own existence at the expense of its commitment to genuine correctional change and to the interests of the community of which it will be a part. Second, its existence will depend considerably on the strength of those alliances that it seeks to build with other correctional change groups and with the community within which it exists. In short, its existence will depend in part on the effectiveness with which it pursues its institutional and social change commitments.

If the reader leaves convinced of nothing else, it must be that the fundamental problem of reentry is the unresponsiveness of our social institutions to the legitimate needs and aspirations of the offender. If we truly expect the released offender to achieve a productive and meaningful life after prison, it is ultimately this character of our society that must be changed. We can therefore no longer make neat distinctions between "service" programs and "social action" programs. If any meaningful change is to occur, those who claim to help the offender reenter society must take responsibility for both serving his individual needs *and* for addressing the institutional sources of his problems. We help support the individual in his struggles with personal adjustment in order to keep our own humanity alive. We join with him in the struggle to change our social institutions because we recognize that ultimately, in a society with as tenuous a commitment to its people as ours, his problems will eventually be our own.

Appendix

Appendix

Table A-1

Correlations Contrasting the Former Addicts (N=21) with the Nonaddicts (N=13) on Various Measures Reflecting Reentry Stress. The Contrasts Are Structured so that the Larger the Correlations, the Greater the Indicated Stress for the Former Addicts.

	Former Addicts v. Nonaddicts
B1 Measures:	
short time hard	.39[a]
depression	.55[b]
excitement	.04
expectancy for success	.07
expect peer trouble	.15
expect family trouble	.06
plans to work	.14
B2 Measures:	
negative emotional reactions	.48[b]
physical symptoms	.46[b]
feel strange	.01
time with peers	.04
family problems	.23
job difficulties	.18
reported progress	−.26
B3 Measures:	
reported progress	−.46[b]
report reentry difficult	.48[b]
feel strange	.38[a]
family problems	.43[b]
job difficulties	.21
time with peers	−.24

[a] $p < .05$
[b] $p < .01$

Table A-2

Correlations of Mothers' Ratings of Expected Postrelease Family Relationship with Her Ratings of Past and Prison Relationships

	Past Relationship	Past Conflict	Prison Relationship
Expected Relationship:	.38[a]	.41[a]	.26
Expected Conflict:	.43[a]	.51[b]	−.19

[a]$p < .05$
[b]$p < .01$

Table A-3

Correlations of Boys' Ratings of Expected Postrelease Family Relationship with His Ratings of Past and Prison Relationships

	Past Relationship	Past Conflict	Prison Relationship
Expected Relationship:	.24	−.16	.47[b]
Expected Conflict:	.07	.06	.46[b]
Expected Mother's Reaction	.36[a]	.40[a]	.14

[a]$p < .05$
[b]$p < .01$

References

References

Bakal, Y. (Ed.) *Closing Correctional Institutions*. Lexington, Mass.: Lexington Books, D.C. Heath & Co., 1973.

Becker, H.S. *Outsiders: Studies in the Sociology of Deviance*. New York: The Free Press, 1963.

Burdman, M. "Realism in Community-Based Correctional Services." in J. Conrad (Ed.) "The Future of Corrections." *Annals of the American Academy of Political and Social Science* 381 (January 1969): 71-80.

Clemmer, D. *The Prison Community*. Boston: The Christopher Publishing House, 1940.

Cloward, R.A. and L.E. Ohlin. *Delinquency and Opportunity*. Glencoe, Ill.: The Free Press, 1961.

Cohen, M. "A Study of Community-Based Correctional Needs in Massachusetts." Document of the Massachusetts Department of Corrections, 1972.

Cohen, A. "The Delinquency Subculture." In Giallombardo (Ed.) *Juvenile Delinquency*. New York: John Wiley & Sons, 1966.

Conrad, J. (Ed.) "The Future of Corrections." *Annals of the American Academy of Political and Social Science* 381 (January 1969).

Corrections, Task Force Report, President's Commission on Law Enforcement and Administration of Justice. U.S. Government Printing Office, 1967.

Cressey, D.R. *The Prison: Theoretical Studies in the Social Organization of the Prison*. New York: Holt, Rinehart & Winston, 1961.

Cressey, D.R. "Prison Organizations." In J.B. March (Ed.), *Handbook of Organizations*. Chicago: Rand McNally & Co., 1965.

Dembo, R. "Recidivism: The "Criminals'" Reaction to "Treatment." *Criminology* (February 1971), pp. 345-56.

Emerson, R.M. *Judging Delinquents*. Chicago: Aldine Publishing Co., 1969.

Erickson, R., W. Crow, L. Zurcher, and A. Connett. *Paroled But Not Free*. New York: Behavioral Publications, 1973.

Forer, Lois. *"No One Will Lissen."* New York: Grosset and Dunlop, 1970.

Garabedian, P.G. and D.C. Gibbons. *Becoming Delinquent: Young Offenders and the Correctional System*. Chicago: Aldine Publishing Co., 1970.

Glaser, D. *The Effectiveness of a Prison and Parole System*. New York: Bobbs Merrill Publishing Co., 1964.

Goldenberg, I. "Alternative Models for the Rehabilitation of the Youthful Offender." In Y. Bakal. (Ed.) *Closing Correctional Institutions*. Lexington, Mass.: Lexington Books, D.C. Heath & Co., 1973, Chapter 7.

Haney, B. and M. Gold. "The Juvenile Delinquent Nobody Knows." *Psychology Today*, September 1973.

Miller, W. "Lower Class Culture as a Generating Milieu of Gang Delinquency." In Giallombardo (Ed.) *Juvenile Delinquency*. New York: John Wiley & Sons, 1966.

Ohlin, L.E. *Sociology and the Field of Corrections.* New York: Russell Sage Foundation, 1956.

Platt, A. "The Rise of the Child-Saving Movement: A Study in Social Policy and Correctional Reform." in J. Conrad. (Ed.) "The Future of Corrections." *Annals of the American Academy of Political and Social Science* 381 (January 1969): 21-38.

Rodman, H. and P. Grams. "Juvenile Delinquency and the Family: A Review and Discussion." In *U.S. Task Force Report: Juvenile Delinquency and Youth Crime.* Washington, D.C.: U.S. Government Printing Office, 1967.

Ryan, W. *Blaming the Victim.* New York: Pantheon, 1971.

Schrag, C. "The Correctional System: Problems and Prospects." In J. Conrad, (Ed.) "The Future of Corrections." *Annals of the American Academy of Political and Social Science* 381 (January 1969).

_____. *Crime and Justice: American Style.* Washington, D.C.: U.S. Government Printing Office, 1971.

Sutherland, E.H. *Principles of Criminology*, prepared by Donald R. Cressey (5th ed.) Chicago: J.B. Lippincott, Co., 1955.

Sykes, G. *The Society of Captives.* New York: Atheneum, 1969.

Szasz, T. "The Myth of Mental Illness." *American Psychologist* 15 (February 1960): 113-18.

Tannenbaum, F. *Crime and the Community.* New York: Ginn & Co., 1938.

Warren, M.Q. "The Community Treatment Project." Presented at the Annual Conference of the Illinois Academy of Criminology, Chicago, Ill., May 14, 1965.

Warren, M.Q. "The Case for Differential Treatment of Delinquents." In J. Conrad, (Ed.) "The Future of Corrections," *Annals of the American Academy of Political and Social Science* 381 (January 1969): 47-59.

Warren, M.Q. "Correctional Treatment in Community Settings." Washington, D.C.: U.S. Government Printing Office, 1972.

Wheeler, S. "Socialization in Correctional Communities." *American Social Review* 26 (1961): 697-712.

_____. *Controlling Delinquency.* New York: John Wiley & Sons, 1968.

_____. Unpublished study on the criminal careers of juvenile offenders. New York: Russell Sage Foundation (in preparation).

_____, and L. Cottrell, Jr. "The Labeling Process." In D.R. Cressey (Ed.) *Delinquency, Crime, and Social Process.* New York: Harper & Row, 1969.

Wilson, J.Q. "The Police and the Delinquent in Two Cities." in S. Wheeler (Ed.), *Controlling Delinquency.* New York: John Wiley & Sons, 1968.

Index

Index

Friends: case study of, 99; and heroin
use, 56, 74, 77; and reentry, 39-40,
54-56, 55t; and transition
experience, 46, 47n, 48-50
Furloughs, 5
"Future of Corrections, The"
(Conrad), 3, 109

"Getting short": psychology of, 28-31
Girlfriend(s): case study of, 101; and
reentry experience, 40, 56
Glaser, D., 9, 31
Goldenberg, I., 110, 111, 117

Halfway house(s), 2, 5
Heroin, 11-12, 57, 60, 80; abstinence
and alienation, 74-75; availability of,
71-72; characteristics of users,
69-70; as coping response, 73-75;
and employment, 76, 78; and family
situation, 78; friends' use of, 56, 74,
77; and life style, 75, 79; and
nonusers, 76; and prerelease
expectations, 70; and reentry
experience, 41, 69-80; and transition
period, 72, 74, 75; and user's family,
83; users and nonusers compared,
77-79

Institutional community programs, 4,
5
Institutions, and change, 64, 67,
109-118. See also Correctional
system

Jobs. See Employment
Juvenile offender, 3-4. See also
Youthful offender

Labeling, concept of, 67
LEAA, 109
Length of stay (LOS), 15, 16t
Lifestyle: changes in, 62, 63; and
heroin use, 79
LSD, 69

Marijuana, 41, 69
Massachusetts, correctional reform in,
3-4
Money, and reentry experience, 58

NIMH, 109
Non-residential programs, 2

Offender: and justice system, 7; and
opportunity structure, 62, 63-64;
perspectives of, 6, 10; psychological
limitations of, 63-64; and
reintegration programs, 6, 116-118
Ohlin, L.E., 8
Opportunity structure, 65; and
offenders, 62, 63-64; and reentry
programs, 114
"Opportunity theory," 8-9

Parole, 5, 27, 63, 67, 72; and
community corrections, 3; defined,
16; and employment, 50, 52;
prerelease preparation for, 26
Parole officer, 36, 101
Peer group. See Friends
Personal change, and reentry
experience, 61-64
Platt, A., 110
Post release experience: and
delinquent involvement, 41; and
employment, 40; expectations,
84-86; and family relations, 41;
fourth week out, 53-60; and friends,
39-40; and heroin, 41, 71-72; and
residence, 40-41; transition period,
43-52. See also Reentry; Transition
experience
Prerelease experience, 23-32; case
study, 96-98; and employment, 26;
expectations, 30, 62, 70, 82; and
families, 26, 82; institutional
characteristics of, 24-28; and parole,
26; and "planned uncertainty," 24;
and planning, 29-30; and probation,
26; and subjective uncertainty,
25-26; and "systems confusion," 24,

About the Author

A. Verne McArthur is Assistant Professor of Psychology at Boston University. He was awarded the Ph.D. by Yale University where he received training in community psychology at the Yale Psycho-Educational Clinic. For the past five years, Dr. McArthur has been involved in research, consultation, and program evaluation directed at the development of effective community-based alternatives in both juvenile and adult corrections. He is associated with the Massachusetts Coalition for Alternatives to Prisons, a coalition including ex-offenders and their families, for whom he is directing a survey of community reentry programs for adult offenders, assessing the programs' viability as alternative approaches to community reintegration.

LIBRARY OF DAVIDSON COLLEGE